WEST
BREAKFAST
AND BRUNCH
RECIPES

BY
BRUCE & BOBBI FISCHER

GOLDEN
WEST ☼
PUBLISHERS

Front cover photo: Peter Ensenberger/Adstock

Text illustrations by Michael Obrenovich

Back cover illustration courtesy of Bear Paw Inn Bed and Breakfast, Winter Park, Colorado

Other books by Bruce and Bobbi Fischer:

>   *Tortilla Lovers Cook Book*
>   *Grand Canyon Cook Book*
>   *Utah Cook Book*

Printed in the United States of America

2nd Printing © 2000

ISBN #1-885590-40-7

Golden West Publishers, Inc.
4113 N. Longview Ave.
Phoenix, AZ 85014, USA
(602) 265-4392

WESTERN BREAKFASTS

TABLE OF CONTENTS

(Continued on next page)

INDEX *(continued from previous page)*

INTRODUCTION

Good Morning!

You've heard the expression "Breakfast is the most important meal of the day." Here in the West that statement rings true, but it means more than nutrition; breakfast sets the mood for the day. From the ranch hand that's been up since dawn to the busy executive on his way to work, breakfast is the reward for the new day.

So many typical standards are broken as untraditional foods find their way onto the breakfast table. Even the breakfast table has changed to create new and interesting spaces to linger and savor your morning meal. Mexican dishes usually reserved for lunch or dinner have found an acceptable niche in the breakfast nook.

From the mountains to the deserts and from Bed and Breakfasts to the campground, Westerners are creating new and hearty recipes to make breakfast a memorable meal instead of a quick fix.

We have had the opportunity to travel extensively throughout the West, which has given us the good fortune of meeting people in many walks of life. We rejoice in the creativity that has been shared with us, as Westerners continue to develop new and exciting breakfast fares. Not willing to settle for just cold cereal and coffee, they have created recipes to soothe the stomach and satisfy the soul.

We offer this collection of zesty breakfast recipes from kind folks throughout the West. Try some for yourself and we know you'll be rewarded for your efforts.

Bruce Fischer   Bobbi Fischer

ACKNOWLEDGEMENTS

We are grateful to all the kind folks who have contributed recipes which have helped to make this book a fantastic collection of creative breakfast recipes.

Many thanks to the following Bed & Breakfast Inns for sharing their wonderful gourmet breakfast meals with us:

Virginia Nemmers, River Run Inn Bed & Breakfast, Salida Colorado; Nancy and Frank O'Neil, Woodland Inn Bed & Breakfast, Woodland Park, Colorado; Roy and Nonnie Fahsholtz, A Bed & Breakfast on Maple Street, Cortez, Colorado; Mary Ann Craig, Scrubby Oaks Bed & Breakfast, Durango, Colorado; Nancy and Michael Conrin, Eagle Cliff House Bed & Breakfast, Estes Park, Colorado; Martha Waterman, Altamira Ranch Bed & Breakfast, Basalt, Colorado; Sue and Rick Callahan, Bear Paw Inn Bed & Breakfast, Winter Park, Colorado; Howard and Lynda Lerner, Red Crags Bed & Breakfast, Manitou Springs, Colorado; Pat and Andy Fejedelem, Our Hearts Inn Old Colorado City Bed & Breakfast, Colorado Springs, Colorado; Gretchen & John Frobeck, Gretchen's Bed & Breakfast, Greer, Arizona; Charlie & Mary J. Bast, White Mountain Lodge, Greer, Arizona.

Thanks to our numerous friends along the road and special thanks to Elin Jeffords, noted restaurant critic and avid gourmet cook.

Bear Paw Inn, Winter Park, Colorado

CEREALS

BAKED OATMEAL

Compliments of Pat and Andy Fejedelem, Innkeepers, Our Hearts Inn Old Colorado City Bed & Breakfast, Colorado Springs, Colorado. Pat tells us, "Guests enjoy this dish very much...even those who don't like traditional oatmeal. They say it's like eating a wonderful oatmeal cookie for breakfast!"

3 cups ROLLED OATS
3/4 cups BROWN SUGAR, packed
2 tsp. BAKING POWDER
1 tsp. SALT
1 cup DRIED FRUITS, raisins, apricots, apples (Pat's favorite)
2 cups EVAPORATED MILK
2 EGGS, slightly beaten
1/2 cup MARGARINE or BUTTER, melted
1/2 cup chopped WALNUTS or PECANS

Mix all dry ingredients together in a large bowl. Add milk to beaten eggs and blend well. Add butter to milk and egg mixture and stir well. Pour liquid mixture into dry ingredients and mix until well blended. Add nuts and combine. Bake in individual 6 oz. ramekins or in one large 13 x 9 buttered baking pan. Bake at 375° for 25 minutes.

Note: This recipe can be mixed together and baked immediately or frozen for later use.

RANCH HANDS' OATMEAL

When you live on a ranch, the days start very early! The chores have to be done; even the animals are fed before you! So when breakfast finally comes, you've got a great big appetite. This is when a satisfying bowl of Ranch Hands' Oatmeal tastes best!

8 cups ROLLED OATS
1/3 cup CORN OIL
2/3 cup HONEY
1 cup chopped ALMONDS
1/4 cup MINI CHOCOLATE CHIPS
1 cup COCONUT FLAKES
1 cup RAISINS
1 cup chopped DATES
3/4 cup WHEAT GERM

Spread oatmeal on the surface of a lightly greased cookie sheet and bake in a 350° oven for 10 minutes. In a bowl, mix oatmeal, corn oil, honey, almonds, chocolate chips and coconut together. Spread mixture in a 9 x 13 pan and return to oven. Bake at 325° for 40 minutes, stirring every 10 minutes. Remove from oven and cool. Combine with raisins, dates and wheat germ, mix well and store in the refrigerator.

Serve with warm milk. Serves 6.

Whoa, Nellie!

FOURTEENER'S GRANOLA

Compliments of Virginia Nemmers, Innkeeper, River Run Inn Bed & Breakfast, Salida, Colorado. Take a step back in time by joining Virginia at this 1892 National Historic Inn. You can enjoy a relaxing sunset on the spacious front porch then awaken to a delicous breakfast. Nancy tells us she has mixed and adapted this recipe from many others to bring to you the best tasting granola in the Southwest!

4 cups ROLLED OATS
1/4 cup BROWN SUGAR
2 tsp. CINNAMON
1/2 cup chopped WALNUTS
1/2 cup shelled SUNFLOWER SEEDS
1/2 cup ORANGE JUICE
2 Tbsp. HONEY
2 Tbsp. VANILLA
1/2 cvup RAISINS
1/2 cup chopped dried CRANBERRIES
1/2 cup chopped dried APRICOTS

In a large bowl, mix together oats, sugar, cinnamon, walnuts and sunflower seeds. Place orange juice, honey and vanilla in a microwaveable bowl and heat for one minute or just until honey is liquefied and mixture can be blended. Pour orange juice mixture over oat mixture and stir well to coat. Spread in a large baking pan. Bake in a preheated 350° oven for 30 minutes (stir every 10 minutes) or until mixture is golden brown. Remove from oven and add raisins, cranberries and apricots. Cool well before storing in a plastic container in refrigerator.

Colorado's large concentration of 14,000-foot mountains challenges hikers from around the world. This granola is a great take-along trail food!

GRAND CANYON GRANOLA

Planning to make the hike to the bottom of the Grand Canyon? Start your day with a bowl of this granola and be sure to take some along to munch on during your hike!

2 1/2 cups ROLLED OATS
1 cup COCONUT FLAKES
1/2 cup WHEAT GERM
1/2 cup SESAME SEEDS
1/2 cup chopped ALMONDS
1/2 cup shelled SUNFLOWER SEEDS
1/2 cup HONEY
1/4 cup SALAD OIL
1/2 cup chopped DATES
1/2 cup RAISINS

In a large mixing bowl, combine oats, coconut, wheat germ, sesame seeds, almonds and sunflower seeds. When thoroughly mixed add honey and oil. Spread into a 13 x 9 x 2 inch baking pan and bake at 250° for 45 minutes. Stir every 15 minutes. Remove from the oven and stir in the dates and raisins. Allow mixture to cool, stirring occasionally to keep from sticking. Once cooled, place granola in a plastic container for storage.

Serve with milk or yogurt and fresh fruit. Serves 2.

FOOT-STOMPIN' SIX GRAIN CEREAL

Start your day with this power-packed breakfast. It will give you energy all day long!

1 cup WHOLE WHEAT
1 cup WHOLE RYE
1 cup WHOLE BARLEY
1 cup BROWN RICE
1 cup MILLET
1 cup GROATS
4 cups WATER
1/2 tsp. SALT
1/2 cup RAISINS
1/2 cup chopped DATES
1 sm. BANANA, sliced

Mix the wheat, rye, barley, rice, millet and groats (oatmeal) together in a large plastic container and store in refrigerator. The day before you want to serve this meal, combine one cup of the mixture with 4 cups of water and let soak overnight in refrigerator. In the morning add salt and bring to a boil. Lower heat and let simmer for one hour or until water is cooked out. Add raisins, dates and banana and serve.

Makes you want to kick yer heals up!

RAISIN GRANOLA

Served with warm milk, this is a great treat on a cold winter morning.

10 cups quick cooking OATS
1 cup WHEAT GERM
1 cup WATER
1/2 cup CORN OIL
2 tsp. SALT
1 cup chopped PECANS
1 cup chopped DATES
1 cup RAISINS

Combine oats and wheat germ in a large bowl. Set aside. Place water, oil, salt, pecans and dates in a blender bowl. Blend until smooth. Combine oat mixture with liquids and blend until smooth. Spread mixture on a cookie sheet. Bake in a 250° oven for 45 minutes, stirring every 10 minutes. Remove from oven and mix in raisins. Serve in bowls with warm milk.

PINE NUT GRANOLA

Great as a cereal, added to other cereals or to take on your hike
for a nourishing trail snack!

1 1/2 cups PINE NUTS (piñon nuts)
4 cups ROLLED OATS
1/2 cups shredded COCONUT
1 cup WHEAT GERM, toasted
1/2 cup VEGETABLE OIL
1/2 cup HONEY

In a large bowl, combine the pine nuts, oats, coconut and wheat germ. Combine oil and honey and work into the oat mixture. Mix well to avoid lumps. Pour mixture into a large shallow pan. Bake in a pre-heated 350° oven for 30 minutes. Stir every 10 minutes. Let granola cool, stirring occasionally. Store in a plastic container in the refrigerator.

DOWNEY HOUSE GRANOLA

Compliments of Downey House Bed & Breakfast, La Conner, Washington. This granola can be served with milk, over yogurt, or over hot applesauce. For a tasty dessert, add whipped cream to applesauce and sprinkle with granola.

4 cups ROLLED OATS
2/3 cup WHEAT GERM
2/3 cup UNSWEETENED BIG FLAKE COCONUT
6 Tbsp. SESAME SEEDS
6 Tbsp. shelled SUNFLOWER SEEDS
1/2 cup chopped RAW CASHEWS or sliced ALMONDS
2/3 cup CORN OIL
1/3 cup HONEY
1 tsp. VANILLA
1/4 tsp. SALT
1/2 cup chopped DRIED FRUIT, or RAISINS

Mix first six ingredients together in a large bowl. In a saucepan, combine corn oil, honey, vanilla and salt. Cook over low heat until honey is melted. Pour over dry mixture and blend thoroughly. Spread on a lightly greased cookie sheet and bake at 300° for 35 to 45 minutes, stirring every 10 minutes. Cool and add fruit. Store in freezer in ziplock bags for ready use.

A'hm ready to chow down now!

SOURDOUGH
SPECIALTIES

SOUTHWESTERN SOURDOUGH STARTER

Sourdough starters act as a leavening and flavoring agent to make bread, pancakes, waffles and biscuits. Two cups of starter mixture can be substituted for each package of yeast called for in a recipe. The original starter mixture can be kept for many years.

2 cups All-PURPOSE FLOUR   **1 pkg. DRY YEAST**
1 Tbsp. SUGAR   **2 cups WARM WATER**

In a large nonmetal bowl, mix together flour, sugar and yeast. Gradually stir in water and mix until smooth. Cover; let stand in a warm place for 48 hours. Store in a covered jar in refrigerator. Stir well before using in recipes. To replenish, mix in 1 cup of flour and 1 cup warm water until smooth. Let stand for a few hours or until mixture bubbles before covering and replacing in refrigerator.

Every week, remove 1 cup starter and use or discard. Replenish as above. Makes 4 cups of starter.

HEARTY SOURDOUGH PANCAKES

For extra-nutty pancakes, substitute 1 cup of granola for the brown sugar in this recipe. A cup of blueberries or other fruit added just before cooking is another favorite variation.

2 cups SOURDOUGH STARTER (p.15)
2 EGGS
2 tsp. BROWN SUGAR
1/4 cup NON-FAT DRY MILK
1 tsp. BAKING SODA

Mix sourdough starter, eggs, sugar and dry milk. Add water or flour to mixture, as needed, for desired consistency. Stir in baking soda and allow to stand for a moment or two. Ladle or pour batter onto greased skillet (cast iron works best). Fry until bubbles form and break on top. Turn and continue frying until golden brown.

SOURDOUGH MUFFINS

1/2 cup SOURDOUGH STARTER (p. 15)
1 cup MILK
2 3/4 cups FLOUR
1 Tbsp. SUGAR
1 tsp. SALT
1/2 tsp. BAKING SODA
CORNMEAL

In a large mixing bowl, combine sourdough, milk and two cups of flour. Mix together, cover and let set at room temperature about eight hours. Mix 1/2 cup flour, sugar, salt and soda. Sprinkle mixture over the dough and mix in thoroughly. Turn dough out onto a board floured with the remaining 1/4 cup flour. Knead two to three minutes. Roll out to 3/4-inch thickness. Use a 3-inch cookie cutter to make nine muffins. Place muffins one inch apart on a cookie sheet, cover with a towel and let rise for an hour. Sprinkle both sides with cornmeal and bake in a 300° oven for 10 minutes. Remove cookie sheet from oven and turn muffins, return to oven for another 10 minutes.

SOURDOUGH BREAD

The cooks on cattle drives depended upon sourdough starters for their breads, biscuits and pancakes. They knew how important a hearty breakfast was to the cowboys heading out on the trail.

1 qt. SOURDOUGH STARTER (p. 15)
1 qt. LUKEWARM WATER
1 cup SUGAR
2 Tbsp. SALT
6 Tbsp. SHORTENING, melted
12 cups FLOUR

Mix starter with water and add the sugar, salt and shortening. Add the flour slowly, kneading until dough is smooth and elastic. Place in a greased bowl and let rise. After the dough has risen, take it out and knead it again and then let it rise again. Shape into four oblong loaves and place on a lightly greased cookie sheet. Cover with foil and set in a warm place. Let dough rise until almost doubled in size. Just before baking, brush the outsides with water and make diagonal slashes across the tops of the loaves with a sharp knife. Bake in a 350° oven for one hour.

SOURDOUGH CORN BREAD

Some people just don't think of cornbread for breakfast.
Try it, you'll like it!

1 cup SOURDOUGH STARTER (p. 15)
1 1/2 cups YELLOW CORNMEAL
1 1/2 cups EVAPORATED MILK
2 EGGS, beaten
2 Tbsp. SUGAR
1/4 cup BUTTER, melted
1/2 tsp. SALT
3/4 tsp. BAKING SODA

Mix the sourdough starter, cornmeal, milk, eggs and sugar thoroughly in a large bowl. Stir in butter, salt and baking soda. Turn into a 10-inch loaf pan and bake at 450° for 30 minutes. Cool on rack.

SOURDOUGH COWBOY BISCUITS

For a taste of the cowboys' life on the prairie, try these!

1 1/2 cups ALL-PURPOSE FLOUR
2 tsp. BAKING POWDER
1/4 tsp. BAKING SODA
1/2 tsp. SALT
1/4 cup BUTTER, melted
1 cup SOURDOUGH STARTER (p. 15)

Sift dry ingredients together. Blend in butter and sourdough starter and mix well. Pat dough out on a floured surface. Cut into 12 rounds or squares and place on greased baking sheets. Cover and let rise 30 minutes. Bake in a 450°oven for 20 minutes or until golden brown.

SOURDOUGH WHEAT MUFFINS

Nutritious, tasty and a great addition to any meal!

1/2 cup WHOLE WHEAT FLOUR
1 1/2 cups ALL-PURPOSE FLOUR
1/2 cup SOURDOUGH STARTER (p. 15)
1/2 cup SUGAR
1 tsp. SALT
1 tsp. BAKING SODA
2 EGGS
1/2 cup SAFFLOWER OIL
1/2 cup EVAPORATED MILK
1 cup RAISINS

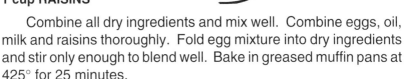

Combine all dry ingredients and mix well. Combine eggs, oil, milk and raisins thoroughly. Fold egg mixture into dry ingredients and stir only enough to blend well. Bake in greased muffin pans at 425° for 25 minutes.

BREADS & MUFFINS

NANCY'S ZUCCHINI BREAD

Compliments of Nancy and Frank O'Neil, Innkeepers, Woodland Inn Bed & Breakfast, Woodland Park, Colorado. Serve Nancy's Zucchini Bread with Frank's Seafood Omelette (p. 44) for the perfect entree!

3 EGGS
1 cup unsweetened APPLESAUCE (replaces oil)
2 cups SUGAR
2 tsp. VANILLA
2 cups shredded ZUCCHINI
1 cup CRUSHED PINEAPPLE, drained
3 cups ALL-PURPOSE FLOUR
2 tsp. BAKING SODA
1 tsp. SALT
1/2 tsp. BAKING POWDER
1 1/2 tsp. CINNAMON
3/4 cup RAISINS
1 cup chopped WALNUTS or PECANS

Beat eggs with applesauce, sugar, and vanilla until fluffy. Stir in zucchini and pineapple. Mix flour, baking soda, salt, baking powder and cinnamon. Add to applesauce mixture. Add raisins and nuts. Pour into two greased and floured loaf pans. Bake at 350° for one hour and 15 minutes. (Freezes well.)

WESTERN BREAKFAST BREAD

Whether frozen or fresh, the strawberries and blueberries make this a very special breakfast treat.

3 cups ALL-PURPOSE FLOUR
1 tsp. SALT
1 tsp. BAKING SODA
1 Tbsp. CINNAMON
2 cups SUGAR
3 EGGS, beaten
1 cup SALAD OIL
2 pkgs. (10 oz. ea.) frozen sliced STRAWBERRIES, thawed
1 pkg. (10 oz.) frozen BLUEBERRIES, thawed
1 cup chopped WALNUTS

In a large bowl, combine flour, salt, baking soda, cinnamon and sugar and mix thoroughly. Create a well in the center of the dry ingredients. Pour the eggs and oil into the well and stir until well combined. Add strawberries, blueberries and walnuts. Mix thoroughly. Pour the mixture into two 8 x 4 greased loaf pans. Bake at 350° for one hour or until loaves test done.

Toast it for an extra taste treat!

PIONEER BREAD

This recipe dates back to the early 1900s when the pioneers came out West. Supplies were meager and they had to make do with what they had. This is a simple yet tasty recipe.

1/2 cup HONEY
1/4 cup BUTTER
2 EGGS, beaten
1 cup WHOLE WHEAT FLOUR
1 tsp. BAKING POWDER
1 1/2 cups shelled SUNFLOWER SEEDS
1 cup MILK
1/4 cup chopped WALNUTS

Combine the honey, butter and eggs. Mix in flour, baking powder and sunflower seeds. Slowly add milk and walnuts. Mix until batter is smooth. Pour into a greased loaf pan and bake at 325° for one hour. Let cool on rack. Serve with orange marmalade or your favorite preserves.

BRAN-BERRY BREAD

Traditionally, cranberries are eaten just at Thanksgiving time, but not out here in the West. Try this bread once and you'll be back for more all year long.

3 EGGS, beaten
1 can (16 oz.) WHOLE CRANBERRY SAUCE
1 1/2 cups BUTTERMILK
1/3 cup SAFFLOWER OIL
3 boxes (8 oz. ea.) BRAN MUFFIN MIX
1/2 cup chopped DATES
1 cup chopped WALNUTS

Combine eggs and cranberry sauce and blend. Stir in buttermilk and oil. Add muffin mixes and stir. Add dates and nuts. Mix again. Pour into two loaf pans. Bake in a 350° oven for one hour. Allow to cool in oven for 15 minutes, then serve. Tastes great with cream cheese and a large glass of apple juice!

CRANBERRY MORNING BREAD

2 1/4 cups ALL-PURPOSE FLOUR
1 cup SUGAR
1/4 tsp. SALT
1 tsp. BAKING POWDER
1 tsp. BAKING SODA
1 cup chopped PECANS
1 cup fresh CRANBERRIES
1/4 cup chopped DATES
2 ORANGE RINDS, grated
2 EGGS
3/4 cup SAFFLOWER OIL
1 cup BUTTERMILK

Sift dry ingredients together. Add nuts, cranberries, dates and orange rind. Combine eggs, oil and buttermilk. Add to flour and fruit mixture. Place in a loaf pan and bake in a preheated oven at 350° for one hour. When bread has cooled, pour *Orange Sauce Topping* over the top. Serve warm with coffee . . . a smooth way to start your day!

ORANGE SAUCE TOPPING

1/2 cup SUGAR
3/4 cup ORANGE JUICE

Dissolve sugar in orange juice.

A great way to start a new day!

PECAN BREAD

3 cups ALL-PURPOSE FLOUR
1 tsp. SALT
1 tsp. BAKING SODA
1 Tbsp. CINNAMON
2 cups SUGAR
3 EGGS, well beaten
1 1/4 cup CORN OIL
1 Tbsp. VANILLA
2 pkgs. (10 oz. ea.) frozen SLICED STRAWBERRIES, thawed
1 1/4 cups chopped PECANS

Combine flour, salt, baking soda, cinnamon and sugar in a large mixing bowl. Mix together well. Create a hole in the center of the mixture. Place the eggs, oil and vanilla in the center. Stir until all ingredients are moistened. Add the strawberries and pecans. Put the batter into two lightly greased bread pans. Sprinkle a few pecans on top and bake in a pre-heated oven at 350° for one hour. Bread is done when knife inserted comes out clean. Allow bread to sit overnight at room temperature.

COWPOKE PUMPKIN BREAD

Served with tea and honey, this is a scrumptious treat!

3 1/2 cups ALL-PURPOSE FLOUR
2 tsp. BAKING SODA
1 1/2 tsp. SALT
1 tsp. CINNAMON
1 tsp. NUTMEG
3 cups SUGAR
1 cup SAFFLOWER OIL
4 EGGS
2/3 cup WATER
2 cups CANNED PUMPKIN
1 cup chopped WALNUTS

Preheat oven to 350°. Sift the flour, soda, salt, cinnamon, nutmeg and sugar together. Add the remaining ingredients and mix well. Pour into 2 greased and floured loaf pans. Bake at 350° for one hour. Let cool on rack.

ROOTIN' TOOTIN' POTATO BREAD

2 pkgs. YEAST
1/2 cup lukewarm WATER
1 1/2 cups scalded MILK
2/3 cup BUTTER
1/2 cup SUGAR
2 tsp. SALT
1 cup mashed POTATOES
6 cups ALL-PURPOSE FLOUR
2 EGGS, beaten
melted BUTTER

Mix yeast and water in a bowl and set aside. Combine milk, butter, sugar, salt and mashed potatoes. Add yeast and 3 cups flour and beat well. Blend in eggs. Gradually add remaining flour to mixture. Turn onto lightly floured surface and knead until smooth. Place in a greased bowl and brush top of dough lightly with butter. Cover and let rise for one hour. Pat and shape into loaf form. Place in greased loaf pan, brush again with melted butter, cover and let set in a warm area for 30 minutes. Bake in a 375° oven for 20 minutes.

Yee hah! It's a new day!

NUTTY LOAF

Top a slice of this bread with peanut butter and serve with a tall cold glass of milk for rave reviews.

1 cup GRANOLA
2 cups BUTTERMILK
3/4 cup SUGAR
2 EGGS, beaten
3 Tbsp. SAFFLOWER OIL
4 cups ALL-PURPOSE FLOUR
1 tsp. BAKING SODA
1/2 tsp. SALT
4 tsp. BAKING POWDER

Mix granola and buttermilk and let stand for 15 minutes. Add sugar and eggs and mix well. Mix in the safflower oil. Sift flour, soda, salt and baking powder together and add to liquid mixture. Mix well. Pour into two greased loaf pans. Cover with a towel and let set in a warm area for 45 minutes. Bake in a 350° oven for one hour. Cool on rack before slicing.

OLD WEST CHEESE LOAF

1/2 cup BUTTER, softened
1 lb. SHARP CHEDDAR CHEESE, grated
1 large loaf of WHOLE GRAIN BREAD, unsliced

Let cheese and butter set at room temperature until both have softened then cream them together. Cut crust from top and sides of loaf, leaving bottom crust intact. Cut loaf lengthwise, then cut crosswise slices. Spread the butter and cheese mixture on all sides of each section. Place loaf in a loaf pan and bake at 350° for 30 minutes. Let cool to room temperature. Serve with your favorite salsa on the side.

JANET'S ZUCCHINI BREAD

Compliments of Pat (and Pat's sister, Janet) and Andy Fejedelem, Innkeepers, Our Hearts Inn Old Colorado City Bed & Breakfast, Colorado Springs, Colorado.

3 lg. EGGS
2 cups GRANULATED SUGAR
1 cup CANOLA OIL
3 tsp. VANILLA FLAVORING
3 cups ALL-PURPOSE FLOUR
1 tsp. CINNAMON
1/4 tsp. NUTMEG
1/2 tsp. BAKING POWDER
1 tsp. BAKING SODA
1 tsp. SALT
1 cup chopped NUTS
1 cup RAISINS
2 cups grated, unpeeled ZUCCHINI

Combine eggs and sugar and beat until fluffy. Add oil and vanilla to mixture. Separately, mix flour, spices, baking powder, baking soda and salt together. Remove 3 tablespoons of flour mixture and stir into nuts and raisins to coat. Mix flour mixture and grated zucchini alternately into the egg mixture. Add the nuts and raisins and stir to mix. Pour into two greased loaf pans and bake in a 350° oven for 1 hour.

Wake up and smell the Zucchini Bread!

DELICIOUS BANANA BREAD

4 Tbsp. BUTTER, softened
2 cups SUGAR
1/2 pt. SOUR CREAM
1 tsp. BAKING SODA
3 BANANAS, mashed
1/2 tsp. SALT
4 EGGS
3 cups ALL-PURPOSE FLOUR
1 cup chopped WALNUTS

Cream together the butter, sugar and sour cream. Add baking soda, bananas, salt and eggs. Mix well. Slowly add the flour and walnuts, stirring constantly. Pour into two 5 x 9 baking pans and bake at 350° for two hours or until center tests done. Cool on racks before slicing.

ORANGE-CINNAMON BREAD

1 1/2 cups ALL-PURPOSE FLOUR
2 tsp. BAKING POWDER
1/2 tsp. BAKING SODA
3/4 cup SUGAR
1/4 tsp. SALT
2 tsp. CINNAMON
1 cup ROLLED OATS
juice from 1 ORANGE
1 cup WATER, boiling
1 EGG, beaten
1/8 cup CORN OIL
1 cup SEEDLESS RAISINS

Sift together flour, baking powder, baking soda, sugar, salt, and cinnamon. Add oats and orange juice. Mix together. Add one cup of boiling water to the mixture and stir untl blended. Combine egg, oil and raisins and stir into mixture. Pour batter into a greased 8 x 4 x 2 bread pan. Bake in 350° oven for one hour. Let bread cool on rack. Serve with orange juice and honey.

FINGER LICKIN' LEMON LOAF

Between the melting chocolate and the tangy taste
of lemon, you won't have any leftovers!

2 1/2 cups ALL-PURPOSE FLOUR
1 tsp. BAKING POWDER
1 tsp. SALT
1 cup BUTTER, softened
1 1/2 cups SUGAR
4 EGGS, slightly beaten
1 cup MILK
2 cups chopped PECANS
2 LEMON RINDS, grated
2 pkgs (6 oz. ea.) semi-sweet CHOCOLATE BITS

In a bowl, mix together the flour, baking powder and salt. In another bowl, cream butter and sugar together. Add eggs, beating lightly. Add flour mixture and milk alternately, blending well after each addition. Stir in nuts, lemon rind, and chocolate bits. Pour into two greased loaf pans. Bake at 350° for one hour. Cool on rack and serve warm.

Finger lickin' good!

HOPI CORN BREAD

1 cup ALL-PURPOSE FLOUR
1 tsp. SALT
1 Tbsp. freshly ground BLACK PEPPER
1 Tbsp. BAKING POWDER
2 Tbsp. SUGAR
3/4 cup CORNMEAL
2 EGGS
1 cup MILK
2 Tbsp. Oil

Sift together the flour, salt, pepper, baking powder and sugar. Add cornmeal. Mix eggs, milk and oil in blender. Add egg mixture to dry ingredients and stir. Mixture will be slightly lumpy. Pour into a greased 9 x 13 baking pan and bake at 425° for 20 minutes.

SONORAN CORN BREAD

2 EGGS, beaten
2/3 cup SAFFLOWER OIL
1/2 cup COTTAGE CHEESE
1 can (16 oz.) CREAMED CORN
1/4 cup MILK
1 cup ALL-PURPOSE FLOUR
1 tsp. SALT
1 tsp. CILANTRO
1 tsp. BAKING POWDER
1/4 cup diced GREEN CHILES

Preheat oven to 350°. Combine eggs, oil, cottage cheese, creamed corn and milk. Mix well. Add flour, salt, cilantro, baking powder and green chiles. Pour mixture into a 9 x 9 baking pan and and bake at 375° for 45 minutes. Serve with salsa on the side.

MESA VERDE CORN BREAD

2 cups ALL-PURPOSE FLOUR
1/2 cup UNCOOKED OATMEAL
1/4 cup GRANULATED SUGAR
2 tsp. BAKING POWDER
1/2 tsp. SALT
1/2 cup BUTTER, melted
2 EGGS
3/4 cup MILK
1 cup FRESH CORN KERNELS
1 Tbsp. diced JALAPEÑOS

Mix flour, oatmeal, sugar, baking powder and salt. Add the butter, eggs, milk, corn and jalapeños. Beat until mixture is thoroughly combined. Pour batter into a 9 x 13 greased baking dish. Bake in a preheated oven at 375 ° for 20 minutes. Let cool on rack.

MORNING CORN BAKE

1/2 cup BUTTER
1 can (16 oz.) WHOLE KERNEL CORN
1 can (16 oz.) CREAM-STYLE CORN
1 pkg. (8 oz.) SOUR CREAM
1 pkg. (8 oz.) CORNBREAD MIX
2 EGGS, beaten

In a large bowl, combine butter, corn and sour cream. Add cornbread mix and stir together well. Pour into a shallow baking pan and bake in preheated oven at 350° for 45 minutes. Halfway through baking, remove pan from oven and press six depressions into the top. Divide beaten egg into depressions. Cover and continue baking 10 minutes or until the eggs are set. Serve warm with salsa on the side. Serves 6.

DESERT PINE NUT MUFFINS

1 cup WHOLE WHEAT FLOUR
1/2 cup WATER
2 tsp. BAKING POWDER
1 cup ground PINE NUTS
3 Tbsp. MESQUITE HONEY
1 tsp. CINNAMON
1 tsp. VANILLA

Combine all ingredients and then pour mixture 2/3 full into lightly greased muffin cups. Bake in a 350° oven for 30 minutes.

RANCH-STYLE RAISIN MUFFINS

As soon as these muffins come out of the oven, get yours quick 'cause they go real fast!

1 cup ALL-PURPOSE FLOUR
1/4 cup SUGAR
3 tsp. BAKING POWDER
1 cup uncooked OATMEAL

3/4 cup RAISINS
1 tsp. OIL
1 EGG, beaten
1 cup MILK

Mix flour, sugar and baking powder together. Add the balance of ingredients and mix thoroughly. Grease 12 muffin cups and fill each 2/3 full with muffin mixture. Add **Brown Sugar Topping** to fill the remainder of the cups. Bake at 425° for 20 minutes.

BROWN SUGAR TOPPING

2 Tbsp. BROWN SUGAR
2 Tbsp. ALL-PURPOSE FLOUR

1 tsp. CINNAMON
1 tsp. BUTTER, melted

Cream sugar, flour and cinnamon and then fold in butter.

PEAR-OATMEAL MUFFINS

Compliments of Charlie and Mary J. Bast, Innkeepers, White Mountain Lodge, Greer, Arizona. "Our lodge overlooks a gorgeous meadow and the Little Colorado River and is surrounded by pine and aspen-covered hills."

1 cup BUTTER or MARGARINE
1 1/2 cups firmly packed BROWN SUGAR
2 EGGS
1 1/2 cups FLOUR
2 cups quick cooking OATS
1 tsp. CINNAMON
2 tsp. BAKING POWDER
1/2 tsp. BAKING SODA
1/2 tsp. SALT
1 1/2 cups diced (very ripe) PEARS
1 cup RAISINS
1/2 cup chopped NUTS

Preheat oven to 350°. Cream butter (or margarine) with brown sugar until light and fluffy. Add eggs and beat well. Add in dry ingredients and mix thoroughly. Blend in pears, raisins and nuts. Spoon 2/3 full into well-greased or lined muffin cups. Bake in 350° oven for 25 to 30 minutes. Cool on a rack.

APPLESAUCE MUFFINS

1/3 cup SAFFLOWER OIL
1/2 cup BROWN SUGAR
1 cup APPLESAUCE
1 tsp. BAKING SODA
1 tsp. CINNAMON

1 1/2 cups WHOLE WHEAT
   FLOUR
1/2 cup RAISINS
1/4 cup chopped WALNUTS

Mix oil, brown sugar and applesauce together in large mixing bowl. Combine baking soda, cinnamon and flour. Add flour mixture to applesauce mixture and stir until smooth. Add raisins and walnuts. Fill greased muffin cups 2/3 full and bake in a 350° oven for 20 minutes.

PUMPKIN MUFFINS

1 cup HONEY
1/2 cup SAFFLOWER OIL
4 EGGS
1 1/2 cups puréed PUMPKIN
3 cups WHOLE WHEAT FLOUR
1 tsp. BAKING SODA
1/2 tsp. ground CLOVES
3/4 tsp. CINNAMON
1/2 tsp. NUTMEG
2 cups RAISINS
1 cup chopped WALNUTS

Mix honey, oil, eggs and pumpkin in large mixing bowl and set aside. Sift together flour, baking soda and spices. Combine flour and pumpkin mixtures together until smooth and fold in raisins and walnuts. Pour mixture 2/3 full into 24 greased muffin cups. Bake at 400° for 20 minutes. Let cool on rack.

SOUTH-OF-THE-BORDER CORN MUFFINS

Serve these muffins with a side of salsa for great western flavor.

1 1/4 cups ALL-PURPOSE FLOUR
3/4 cup CORNMEAL
2 Tbsp. SUGAR
4 tsp. BAKING POWDER
1/2 tsp. SALT
3/4 cup MILK
1/4 cup SOUR CREAM
1/4 cup OIL
1 EGG
1 can (4 oz.) diced GREEN CHILES

In a large bowl, combine flour, cornmeal, sugar, baking powder and salt. Mix well. In a medium bowl, combine milk, sour cream, oil, egg and chiles and mix thoroughly. Add milk mixture to dry ingredients, stirring until mixture is moist and smooth. Pour into 12 greased muffin cups 2/3 full and bake at 400° for 20 minutes.

BRUNCH

CREAM CHEESE CROISSANTS & FRESH PEACH STRATA

Compliments of Pat and Andy Fejedelem, Innkeepers, Our Hearts Inn Old Colorado City Bed & Breakfast, Colorado Springs, Colorado. "This makes a wonderful breakfast side dish as well as a scrumptious dessert dish."

2-3 ripe FRESH PEACHES, peeled
1 cup SUGAR, divided
1/2 tsp. NUTMEG
1/2 tsp. CINNAMON
2-3 lg. CREAM CHEESE CROISSANTS
4 extra-lg. EGGS
1 1/2 cups WHOLE MILK or 1/2 cup WHOLE MILK
    and 1 cup HALF & HALF
1 tsp. PURE VANILLA EXTRACT
VANILLA YOGURT

Slice peaches into a large glass bowl and sprinkle with a mixture of 1/2 cup sugar, nutmeg and cinnamon. Set aside. Slice cream cheese croissants into 1" slices and layer in a deep baking dish with cream cheese side up. Spoon peaches over croissant slices. Add a second layer of croissant slices on top. Whisk eggs, milk, 1/2 cup sugar and vanilla extract together until smooth. Pour egg mixture over the layered croissants and peaches. Let mixture set for one-half hour so that egg mixture will be absorbed. Sprinkle top with additional nutmeg and bake at 350° for one hour until set and golden brown. Garnish with vanilla yogurt and fresh peach slices.

FRENCH TOAST STRATA

Compliments of Mary Ann Craig, Innkeeper, Scrubby Oaks Bed & Breakfast, Durango, Colorado. Mary Ann says, "Breakfasts at Scrubby Oaks is a 'happening' where you can meet travelers from all over the world!" Each day, Mary Ann offers guests an array of fruits, juices, homemade breads, jams, jellies and unforgettable gourmet entrées.

1 lb. (12 cups) cubed FRENCH BREAD
1 pkg. (8 oz.) CREAM CHEESE, cubed
8 EGGS, beaten
2 1/2 cups MILK
6 Tbsp. MARGARINE, melted
1/4 cup MAPLE SYRUP
GROUND NUTMEG, to taste

Grease a 13 x 9 baking pan. Place one half of bread cubes in the pan. Top with cream cheese cubes and remaining bread cubes. Combine eggs, milk, melted margarine and maple syrup. Beat until well blended. Pour egg mixture evenly over the bread and cheese cubes. Using a spatula, lightly press layers down to moisten. Sprinkle nutmeg over all. Cover with plastic wrap and refrigerate overnight. In the morning, remove plastic wrap. Bake, uncovered, in a 325° oven for 35-40 minutes or until center appears set and edges are lightly golden. Let stand 10 minutes before serving. Cut into squares and serve with warm maple or raspberry syrup.

Ooh la la!

CHOCOLATE CROISSANT STRATA

Compliments of Pat and Andy Fejedelem, Innkeepers, Our Hearts Inn Old Colorado City Bed & Breakfast, Colorado Springs, Colorado. Pat and Andy say, "A nostalgic glimpse of the past awaits you. Just imagine a summer's garden or a winter's glowing fire beckoning you to linger a bit and experience why 'Our Hearts are Inn Old Colorado City.'"

3 lg. CHOCOLATE CROISSANTS
2-3 lg. EGGS, lightly beaten
1 1/2 cups CHOCOLATE MILK or substitute chocolate syrup
**   and milk mixture**
grated BITTERSWEET or other CHOCOLATE
WHIPPED CREAM or VANILLA YOGURT, for garnish
STRAWBERRIES, for garnish

Slice croissants diagonally so chocolate center shows and place in 4 oz. ramekins. Mix eggs and chocolate milk together and pour over top of croissant slices. Bake at 350° for approximately 1 hour. Croissants will puff and eggs will be set. Remove from oven and cool on a wire rack. Sprinkle with grated chocolate immediately. When cooled, add a spoonful of whipped cream (or vanilla yogurt) to each ramekin and place a fan of sliced strawberries on the tops. Sprinkle with additional grated chocolate if desired.

PUFFED CROISSANTS

Compliments of Nancy and Michael Conrin, Innkeepers, Eagle Cliff House Bed& Breakfast, Estes Park, Colorado. Nancy and Michael are hiking and backpacking consultants who love to share their outdoor expertise as well as the home-like amenities and culinary delights of their establishment with their pampered guests.

6 CROISSANTS
1 pkg. (4 oz.) CREAM CHEESE
6 slices TURKEY, HAM or BACON
6 slices ONION
6 slices GREEN BELL PEPPER
6 slices TOMATO

Batter:
  6 EGGS
  1/4 cup PARMESAN CHEESE
  1 cup COTTAGE CHEESE
  1 tsp. CUMIN
  1 tsp. RED CHILI POWDER

Split croissants and spread with a thin layer of cream cheese. Add slices of meat and vegetables. Close croissants like a sandwich. Next, combine eggs, cheeses and spices and stir until well mixed. Dip croissants in batter. Place croissants in a microwave dish and pour remaining batter over the top. Microwave on HIGH for 90-seconds, and continue cooking in 20-second intervals until eggs are cooked and puffy.

Come and get it!

CARAMEL FRENCH TOAST

Compliments of Nonnie and Roy Fahsholtz, Innkeepers, A Bed & Breakfast on Maple Street, Cortez, Colorado. Try this recipe yourself, or spend a night with the Fahsholtz's and enjoy it firsthand.

32 slices WHEAT BREAD
2/3 cup MARGARINE
4 Tbsp. CORN SYRUP
2 cups BROWN SUGAR
1/2 cup WATER
2/3 cup DRY MILK
2 tsp. VANILLA
10 EGGS
2 cups PLAIN YOGURT
2 cups SOUR CREAM
sliced STRAWBERRIES or PEACHES

Just for you, monsieur!

Cut crusts off bread and set aside. Bring the following ingredients to boil: margarine, corn syrup and brown sugar. Stir until well blended. Pour liquid into two 9 x 13 pans. Place bread in two layers in each pan, pressing as needed to fit. In blender, add one half of the water, dry milk, vanilla and eggs; blend just until well combined. Pour mixture over the bread in one of the pans. Add the remaining half of the ingredients together in blender and blend. Pour over the second pan. Cover the pans with plastic wrap and refrigerate one hour or overnight. Bake uncovered at 350° for 45 minutes. Loosen sides and invert onto serving plates (must work fast while caramel is still hot).

Mix yogurt and sour cream. Place two tablespoons of mixture on each serving. Garnish with sliced strawberries or peaches. Serves 16.

COTTAGE CHEESE PANCAKES

6 EGGS, beaten
2 cups small curd, creamed COTTAGE CHEESE
1/2 cup ALL-PURPOSE FLOUR
2 Tbsp. BUTTER, melted
1 tsp. SALT

Combine all ingredients in a mixing bowl. For each pancake, ladle approximately 1/4 cup batter onto hot, well-greased griddle. Cook until pancake center is no longer moist before turning. Flip and brown the other side. Makes 12 pancakes. Serve hot with your favorite topping or preserves (see pages 79 through 82).

OVEN-BAKED FRENCH TOAST

1/2 cup WATER
1/4 cup APPLE JUICE
1/2 cup CASHEWS
2 Tbsp. frozen ORANGE JUICE CONCENTRATE
1 sm. APPLE, finely diced
8 slices SOURDOUGH BREAD, thickly sliced
1 Tbsp. CINNAMON

Place water, apple juice, cashews, orange juice concentrate, and apple in a blender and liquefy all. Pour into a large mixing bowl. Dip slices of bread into mixture until thoroughly soaked. Place bread slices on lightly greased baking sheets and bake in a 400° oven for 10 minutes. Turn slices, dust with cinnamon and bake for another 10 minutes or until golden brown. Serves 4. Serve hot with your favorite topping or preserves (see pages 79 through 82).

BEAR PAW BLINTZ SOUFFLÉ

Compliments of Sue and Rick Callahan, Innkeepers, Bear Paw Inn Bed & Breakfast, Winter Park, Colorado. Rick and Susan Callahan know just what their guests like! From delicious morning gourmet surprises like this, to featherbeds, jacuzzis and spectacular views of Rocky Mountain National Park.

8-9 frozen CHERRY or BLUEBERRY BLINTZES
1/2 cup BUTTER, melted
6 EGGS, beaten
2 cups SOUR CREAM
5 Tbsp. ORANGE JUICE
1 Tbsp. VANILLA
2 tsp. SUGAR

Lay frozen blintzes in a 2-quart baking dish or deep quiche pan. Pour melted better over all. In a separate bowl, combine eggs, sour cream, orange juice, vanilla and sugar and whisk briskly for a few moments. Pour over blintz mixture. Cover with plastic wrap and store in refrigerator overnight. In the morning, remove wrap, bake in preheated 350° oven for approximately 75 minutes. Serves 6.

ORANGE JUICE WAFFLES

3 cups ALL-PURPOSE FLOUR	6 EGGS, separated
2 Tbsp. BAKING POWDER	1 cup ORANGE JUICE
1 tsp. CINNAMON	1 1/2 cups LIGHT CREAM
1 tsp. SALT	1/2 cup BUTTER, melted
2 tsp. SUGAR	2 tsp. grated ORANGE RIND

In a large bowl, mix together flour, baking powder, cinnamon, salt and sugar. Set aside. In a large bowl, beat egg yolks until light in color. Stir into beaten yolks the orange juice, cream, butter and orange rind. Add to dry ingredients and combine. Beat egg whites until stiff peaks form and fold into mixture. Bake in waffle iron. Makes six waffles. Serve with your favorite topping (see pages 79 through 82).

EGGS CALLAHAN

Compliments of Sue and Rick Callahan, Innkeepers, Bear Paw Inn Bed & Breakfast, Winter Park, Colorado. Sue and Rick are the creators of this savory dish. Imagine waking to the aroma of this mouth-watering quiche, enjoying its marvelous flavor and then spending your day in Winter Park.

1 pkg. (16 oz.) frozen, shredded HASH BROWNS, thawed
NONSTICK SPRAY
1/2 cup BUTTER
2 cups shredded CHEDDAR CHEESE
1/2 lb. cooked ITALIAN SAUSAGE
1 cup diced YELLOW BELL PEPPER
1 cup diced RED BELL PEPPER
2 cups diced MUSHROOMS
5 EGGS
1/2 cup MILK
SALT and PEPPER to taste
sliced TOMATOES
sliced AVOCADO
SALSA

Press the thawed hash browns between paper towels to remove moisture. Spray quiche pan with nonstick spray. Press hash browns into pan forming a crust and brush with butter. Bake at 450° for 30 minutes. Remove crust from oven and sprinkle with cheddar cheese. Spread sausage, peppers and mushrooms in crust. Beat together eggs with milk and add salt and pepper. Pour egg mixture over ingredients in crust. Bake uncovered at 350° for 30-40 minutes. Slice and serve with tomatoes, avocado and salsa on the side.

Sue tells us she had a contest when she first opened; guests had to vote on the most suitable egg dish to warrant the name "Eggs Callahan." A couple from Dallas won when they announced to the entire breakfast table that "this has got to be 'Eggs Callahan', Sue, it's so spicy, just like you!" Guests love the dish and the story, too!

FRANK'S SEAFOOD OMELETTE

Compliments of Nancy and Frank O'Neil, Innkeepers, Woodland Inn Bed & Breakfast, Woodland Park, Colorado. Nestled in the foothills of Pikes Peak, the Woodland Inn offers both delicious food and breathtaking views!

8 GREEN ONIONS, chopped
2 cups sliced fresh MUSHROOMS
2 Tbsp. BUTTER or MARGARINE
12 med. SHRIMP, cooked and halved lengthwise
8 oz. cooked or IMITATION CRAB MEAT
1/2 cup SOUR CREAM
8 EGGS
1/2 cup grated SWISS CHEESE

Sauté onions and mushrooms in butter or margarine until soft. Add seafood and sour cream; stir together and warm over very low temperature (do not boil!). Set aside. Whip eggs, two at a time, and pour into a buttered 8-inch omelette pan over medium-high heat. Lift edges frequently to allow uncooked portion to flow underneath. Sprinkle one quarter to one half cup of cheese over center portion on the omelette. Cover and cook until egg mixture is set (about two minutes). Add seafood mixture and fold omelette over . Slide onto a warm plate and garnish the top with halved shrimp and a sprig of parsley. Serve with fresh fruit and hot muffins or **Nancy's Zucchini Bread** (see page 20).

Serves 4.

SPINACH, MUSHROOM & CHEESE QUICHE

Compliments of Lynda and Howard Lerner, Innkeepers, Red Crags Bed & Breakfast, Manitou Springs, Colorado. Join Lynda and Howard in the dining room of their four-story Victorian mansion to enjoy this wonderful dish!

1 pkg. (10 oz.) frozen chopped SPINACH
1/4 tsp. SALT
1/8 tsp. BLACK PEPPER
1 Tbsp. HORSERADISH
4 oz. SOUR CREAM
1 PASTRY SHELL
1/2 lb. MUSHROOMS, sliced
1 Tbsp. BUTTER
2 oz. CHEDDAR CHEESE, grated
3 Tbsp. grated PARMESAN CHEESE
4 EGGS, beaten
1 1/2 cups HALF AND HALF
1/8 tsp. SALT
1/8 tsp. CAYENNE PEPPER
1/8 tsp. NUTMEG

Cook spinach according to package directions. Drain and dry on paper towels. Place spinach in a bowl and blend in salt, pepper, horseradish and sour cream. Spread spinach mixture in pastry shell. Sauté mushrooms in butter, drain and then layer on top of the spinach mixture. Sprinkle mushrooms with grated cheeses. Combine eggs, half and half, and remaining seasonings and beat until smooth. Pour the egg mixture over top of cheeses. Bake in preheated 375° oven for 40 minutes or until the top is puffed up and browned. Test center for doneness. Remove from the oven and let stand for about 10 minutes to set. Serves 6.

TORTILLA SWIRLS

Compliments of Nancy and Frank O'Neil, Innkeepers, Woodland Inn Bed & Breakfast, Woodland Park, Colorado. Nancy sends these swirls along as part of the Field Breakfast for the pilot and crew of their hot air balloon, "High Time." Guests of the Woodland Inn can participate in a special Crew Package, and enjoy the Field Breakfast as well.

1 pkg. (8 oz.) CREAM CHEESE
1 can (4 oz.) diced GREEN CHILES
chopped PIMENTO
chopped RADISHES
chopped BLACK OLIVES
3 FLOUR TORTILLAS

Place cream cheese in a medium-sized microwave-safe bowl. Microwave on medium setting for 30 to 40 seconds just to soften cheese. Stir in chiles, pimentos, radishes and olives and mix well. Spread mixture on tortillas and roll jelly-roll style. Wrap rolled tortillas in plastic wrap and cool in refrigerator for about an hour. Remove and slice into one-inch sections. Put swirls in plastic bags for snacking, or serve as appetizers.

GREEN CHILE RICE

This makes a great side dish to serve with eggs.

4 cups COOKED RICE
1 can (4 oz.) diced GREEN CHILES
1 can (4 oz.) PIMENTOS
1 sm. RED BELL PEPPER, chopped
1 cup SOUR CREAM
1 tsp. SALT
1/2 cup grated CHEDDAR CHEESE
1/2 cup grated MONTEREY JACK CHEESE

In a large bowl mix all ingredients until well blended. Spread mixture in a greased 9 x 9 baking dish and bake for 35 minutes at 350°. Serve hot.

WRANGLER'S SPICY APPLE TREAT

A hearty mid-morning trail snack or serve it warm as a coffeecake.
This treat will keep 'em filled with energy all day long!

1 cup WHOLE WHEAT PASTRY FLOUR
1 tsp. BAKING SODA
1 tsp. SALT
1 tsp. CINNAMON
1/2 tsp. NUTMEG
1/2 tsp. ground CLOVES
1/2 cup BUTTER
3/4 cup DARK BROWN SUGAR
2 EGGS
2 APPLES, coarsely grated
1 cup WHOLE WHEAT FLOUR
1/4 cup BUTTERMILK
1/2 cup chopped ALMONDS

Mmmm, good grub!

Sift together 1 cup pastry flour, baking soda, salt and spices and set aside. In a bowl, cream butter, sugar and eggs together. Stir in grated apples and the second cup of flour. Add buttermilk and blend well. Add sifted dry ingredients and stir until well mixed. Place in a greased round 9-inch baking pan. Spread nuts over top. Bake at 350° for one hour. Let cool on rack.

SWEET TOAST

Kids of all ages will love this for breakfast!

2 Tbsp. frozen ORANGE JUICE CONCENTRATE, thawed
1/2 cup SUGAR
2 tsp. CINNAMON
2 Tbsp. BUTTER, melted
6 slices WHITE BREAD

Preheat broiler. Combine orange juice concentrate, sugar, cinnamon and butter. Place bread on broiler pan and toast lightly on one side. Turn bread and brush with orange juice mixture. Toast for 3 minutes or until lightly browned.

TAMALE PIE

1 sm. ONION, diced	1 can (16 oz.) CORN
1 clove GARLIC, minced	2 tsp. SALT
3 Tbsp. BUTTER	2 tsp. CHILI POWDER
1 Tbsp. CORN OIL	1 cup CORNMEAL
1 lb. lean GROUND BEEF	1 cup MILK
1/2 lb. SAUSAGE	1 cup grated CHEDDAR
1 can (24 oz.) diced TOMATOES	CHEESE

In a large skillet, sauté onion and garlic in butter and oil until tender. Add ground beef and sausage and cook until meats are browned. Let simmer for 30 minutes. Add tomatoes, corn, salt and chili powder and mix well. Drain mixture and pour into a 2-quart baking dish. Mix cornmeal with milk and spread over meat mixture. Sprinkle cheese over top. Bake at 350° for one hour. Serve warm, with salsa on the side. Serves 6.

CHILE EGG PUFF

Compliments of Martha Waterman, Innkeeper, Altamira Ranch Bed & Breakfast, Basalt, Colorado. Imagine enjoying this delicious breakfast while surrounded by 180 acres of Rocky Mountain country bordered by a gold-medal trout stream, the Roaring Fork!

10 EGGS, beaten
1/2 cup ALL-PURPOSE FLOUR
1 tsp. BAKING POWDER
1/2 tsp. SALT
1 pt. small curd COTTAGE CHEESE
4 cups (1 lb.) shredded MONTEREY JACK CHEESE
1/2 cup MARGARINE or BUTTER, melted & cooled
2 can (4 oz. ea.) diced GREEN CHILES

Grease a 9 x 13 baking dish. In a large bowl, beat eggs until light and lemon-colored. Add flour, baking powder, salt, cottage cheese, Jack cheese and butter. Mix until smooth. Stir in chiles until well mixed. Pour into greased baking dish and bake in 350° oven about 35 minutes or until top is browned and center is firm. Serve at once. Serves 8.

GREEN CHILE-EGG PIE

2 Tbsp. BUTTER
2 cans (4 oz. ea.) diced
   GREEN CHILES
3 EGGS, beaten
1 tsp. SALT

1 tsp. ground BLACK PEPPER
1/2 cup grated JACK CHEESE
1/2 cup grated CHEDDAR CHEESE
1/4 cup diced BLACK OLIVES
1/4 cup diced MUSHROOMS

Grease sides and bottom of a 9 x 12 baking dish with butter. Line the bottom and sides with green chiles. In a large bowl, combine remaining ingredients well. Pour over chiles. Bake in a 350° oven for 30 minutes or until top starts to brown. Let cool before serving. Serves 4.

CHARLIE'S
EGG-POTATO PIE

Compliments of Charlie and Mary J. Bast, Innkeepers,
White Mountain Lodge, Greer, Arizona.

3 Tbsp. VEGETABLE OIL
5-6 med. POTATOES, peeled and diced
1/2 cup chopped ONION
1/2 tsp. each: SALT, PEPPER and GARLIC
8 EGGS, beaten
1 cup MILK
1 1/2 cups shredded CHEDDAR CHEESE
1 can (4 oz.) diced GREEN CHILES

Place oil in a skillet and add potatoes, onions, salt, pepper and garlic. Cook over medium heat, stirring occasionally. In a bowl, combine eggs, milk, cheese and chiles and beat thoroughly with an electric mixer. When potatoes are fully cooked, pour egg mixture over them. Carefully mix egg mixture with the potatoes in the skillet so that all is uniform. Cover and cook about 30 minutes over medium-low heat until eggs are done. Cut into pie-shaped wedges and serve.

SAUSAGE 'N' EGG CASSEROLE

10 slices WHITE BREAD
2 cups grated SHARP CHEDDAR CHEESE
1 lb. PORK SAUSAGE, browned
4 EGGS
3/4 tsp. DRY MUSTARD
2 3/4 cups MILK, divided
1 can (10.75 oz.) CREAM OF MUSHROOM SOUP

Remove crusts and cube bread. Place in a greased 9 x 10 casserole dish. Add cheese and browned sausage. Beat eggs, mustard and 2 1/4 cups milk together and pour over top. Let sit in refrigerator overnight. When ready to cook, mix soup and 1/2 cup of milk together and pour on top of mixture. Bake, uncovered, in a 300° oven for 1 1/2 hours. Serve warm with salsa. Serves 4.

BREAKFAST TROUT

1 can (15 oz.) TOMATO SAUCE
1/4 cup BUTTER
1/4 cup chopped ONIONS
2 Tbsp. LEMON JUICE
1/2 cup BEER
1 tsp. SUGAR
1 tsp. SALT
6 TROUT
12 slices lightly cooked BACON

Combine tomato sauce, butter, onions, lemon juice, beer, sugar and salt in a small pan and let simmer for 15 minutes. Wrap each fish in bacon, holding bacon in place with toothpicks. Cook on a grill for about 5 minutes or until the fish flakes easily. Brush sauce over fish before serving. Serve warm sauce on the side. Serves 6.

HUEVOS RANCHEROS

This popular breakfast dish is served at most Mexican restaurants.
It is also served for lunch or dinner.

4 EGGS
2 FLOUR TORTILLAS
1/2 cup CHEDDAR CHEESE
1/4 cup diced ONION
1/2 cup cooked PINTO BEANS
GREEN CHILE SALSA
1/2 cup shredded MONTEREY JACK CHEESE
1/2 cup diced TOMATO

Cook eggs, over easy, in a lightly greased frying pan. While the eggs are cooking, heat tortillas in a large pan over low heat. Divide and spread the cheddar cheese, onion, pinto beans and salsa on the tortillas. Place eggs on tortillas and top with salsa, Jack cheese and tomato. Serve warm with red salsa on the side.

CHEESE SOUFFLÉ

1/2 cup ALL-PURPOSE FLOUR
1 tsp. BAKING POWDER
1/2 tsp. SALT
10 EGGS, well beaten
1 lb. small curd COTTAGE CHEESE
1 lb. MONTEREY JACK CHEESE, grated
1/2 cup BUTTER, melted
2 cans (4 oz. ea.) diced GREEN CHILES

Sift together flour, baking powder and salt. Combine eggs, cottage cheese, Jack cheese, butter and chiles. When well blended, fold in flour mixture. Stir until thoroughly mixed. Pour into a round baking dish and bake at 350° for 40 minutes or until the center is firm. Serves 6.

DOUBLE B RANCH HASH

1 lb. GROUND BEEF
3 lg. RED ONIONS, diced
1 lg. GREEN BELL PEPPER, chopped
1 can (16 oz.) STEWED TOMATOES
1/2 cup MUSHROOMS
1 cup cooked RICE
1/2 cup medium hot SALSA
1 tsp. CHILI POWDER
2 tsp. SALT
1 tsp. BLACK PEPPER

Brown beef in a large frying pan. Drain off excess fat. Add onions and green pepper and sauté until translucent. Add remaining ingredients. Combine well and then pour mixture into a 2-quart casserole dish. Bake at 350° for one hour. Serve with cornbread and butter. Serves 4.

BREAKFAST PIZZA

'Atsa mighty fine pizza!

6 slices WHITE BREAD
4 EGGS
2 Tbsp. MILK
1 tsp. SALT
1 tsp. PEPPER
6 slices CANADIAN BACON
1/2 cup sliced MUSHROOMS
1 cup grated CHEDDAR CHEESE

Remove crusts from bread and place slices in a greased 9-inch square pan. Combine eggs, milk, salt and pepper. Place Canadian bacon, mushrooms and cheese on top of the bread. Pour egg mixture over all. Bake in a preheated 350° oven for 20 minutes or until all the cheese is melted. Serves 4.

ORANGE LENTILS

Compliments of The Surgeon's House Bed and Breakfast, Jerome, Arizona. This recipe makes a great breakfast side dish, or a hearty stuffed pepper brunch.

2 Tbsp. BUTTER
1/4 cup OLIVE OIL
2 Tbsp. SESAME SEED OIL
1 bunch GREEN ONIONS, chopped
1 cup finely chopped MUSHROOMS
1 lg. YELLOW BELL PEPPER,
    finely chopped
2 cups ORANGE LENTILS
1 cup chopped PECANS
1 Tbsp. GREEK SEASONING
1/3 cup chopped fresh CILANTRO
2 cups cheap PINK WINE

In a large pot, over medium heat, melt and combine the butter and oils. Sauté onions, mushrooms and pepper until onion is translucent. Add lentils, pecans, Greek seasoning, cilantro and wine. Bring to a low boil and cover and simmer about 25 minutes or until lentils are tender.

ORANGE LENTIL STUFFED PEPPERS

3 RED BELL PEPPERS
ORANGE LENTIL MIXTURE, above
SMOKED GOUDA, shredded
1 cup cheap PINK WINE

Cut peppers in half lengthwise and fill with lentil mixture. Sprinkle gouda cheese over each. Place in a baking pan and add wine to bottom of pan. Cover and bake for 45 to 60 minutes at 350°.

GRETCHEN'S INCREDIBLE BACON PIE

Compliments of Gretchen & John Forbeck, Gretchen's Bed & Breakfast, Greer, Arizona. "What an aroma this makes while baking! Great to make the night before and prepare for morning guests."

12 slices BACON, fried until crispy
1 cup grated SWISS CHEESE
1/3 cup chopped ONION
2 cups MILK
1 cup BISCUIT MIX
4 EGGS
1/4 tsp. SALT
1/8 tsp. PEPPER

Spray or grease a 10-inch glass pie pan.* Sprinkle crumbled bacon, cheese and onion in bottom of pan. Combine all other ingredients together and pour into pie pan. Bake at 400° for 35 to 40 minutes. Check center for doneness with a knife or toothpick.

*If using a 9-inch pie pan, reduce amounts of milk to 1 1/2 cups, biscuit mix to 3/4 cup and eggs to 3.

Note: Extend baking time 10-15 minutes if it has been refrigerated.

PUFFED EGG SHELLS

1 pkg. PUFF PASTRY SHELLS
6 slices cooked HAM
1 can (4 oz.) diced GREEN CHILES, diced
6 EGGS
1/2 cup CREAM CHEESE, melted
PAPRIKA, to taste
1 ORANGE, sliced

Prepare puff pastry shells according to package directions. Place a slice of ham and one-half teaspoon of green chiles into each shell. Poach eggs and layer one egg on top of each slice of ham. Top with melted cream cheese. Add a dash of paprika to taste. Garnish with orange slices. Serves 3 to 6.

POTATO-TOMATO SUNRISE!

4 POTATOES
1 Tbsp. OIL
1 tsp. GARLIC SALT
1 Tbsp. PAPRIKA
1 Tbsp. freshly ground BLACK PEPPER
1/2 cup diced ONION
1/2 cup CREAM CHEESE, softened
1 lg. TOMATO, chopped
1 cup grated MONTEREY JACK
    CHEESE
1 can (4 oz.) diced GREEN CHILES
1/2 cup whole BLACK OLIVES
4 EGGS, beaten
1 Tbsp. SALT
FLOUR TORTILLAS
SALSA

Time to rise 'n' shine!

Peel, slice and boil potatoes until just done but still firm. Heat oil, garlic, paprika, pepper, onions and potatoes in a large skillet over medium heat. Add cream cheese, tomatoes, cheese, green chiles and olives to potatoes. Let simmer on low heat for 5 minutes. Mix eggs with salt then pour over potatoes. Cover and let stand for 5 minutes on low heat or until eggs are done. Serve with warm tortillas and salsa. Serves 4.

BACON-CHEESE QUICHE

8 slices BACON, cooked
1 cup grated SWISS CHEESE
1 cup chopped MUSHROOMS
2 SCALLIONS, chopped
2 cups MILK

4 EGGS
1 cup BISCUIT MIX
1 tsp. SALT
1 tsp. PEPPER

In a greased pie plate, layer bacon, cheese, mushrooms, and scallions. In a bowl, combine milk, eggs, biscuit mix, salt and pepper. Stir until blended and pour over bacon mixture. Bake at 400° for 45 minutes. Serve with salsa on the side. Serves 4.

HAM WITH APRICOTS

1 med. HAM, cooked and sliced
WHOLE CLOVES
1/2 cup BROWN SUGAR
1 Tbsp. CINNAMON
1 can (15 oz.) peeled WHOLE APRICOTS

Slice ham slices into diamond shaped pieces and place cloves on each piece. Place in a baking pan and sprinkle with brown sugar and cinnamon. Drain the syrup from apricots and pour half of the syrup over the ham pieces. Bake in a 325° oven for one hour. Use syrup in pan to baste every 15 minutes. After one hour place apricots over ham pieces and bake for an additional 15 minutes. Serve warm with syrup on the side. Serves 4.

HASH BROWN CASSEROLE

2 lbs. frozen HASH BROWNS, thawed
1 tsp. SALT
1 tsp. ground PEPPER
1/4 cup chopped ONIONS
1/4 cup diced RED BELL PEPPER
2 cups SOUR CREAM
1 can (10.75 oz.) CREAM OF CHICKEN SOUP
2 cups grated CHEDDAR CHEESE
2 cups crushed CORN FLAKES
1/4 cup BUTTER, melted

Preheat oven to 350°. Combine hash browns, salt, pepper onions, bell pepper, sour cream, soup and cheese. Pour mixture into a greased 4-quart baking dish and bake for 30 minutes. Combine the corn flakes and butter and sprinkle on top of casserole. Bake for an additional 20 minutes. Serves 4.

COLORADO SUNSHINE STRAWBERRIES

2 sticks BUTTER
2 Tbsp. SUGAR
1 1/2 cups ALL-PURPOSE FLOUR
1 pkg. (6 oz.) CREAM CHEESE, softened
2 cups POWDERED SUGAR
1 cup chopped PECANS
1 cup boiling WATER
1 pkg. (3 oz.) STRAWBERRY GELATIN
2 pkgs. frozen STRAWBERRIES (reserve some for garnish)
1 cup NON-DAIRY TOPPING

Mix one stick of butter with sugar and flour until smooth. Spread mixture in greased 9 x 13 baking dish and bake at 350° for 30 minutes. Let cool. Mix remaining stick of butter with cream cheese and powdered sugar until smooth. Spread on top of first mixture. Sprinkle with pecans and set aside. In a bowl, combine boiling water with gelatin and frozen strawberries. When strawberries are defrosted and gelatin has dissolved, mix and pour over mixture in baking dish. Refrigerate at least 1 hour or until ready to serve. Add topping and garnish with reserved strawberries. Serves 4 to 6.

APPLE GOLDEN CRISP

8 APPLES
1/3 cup ORANGE JUICE
   CONCENTRATE
1/3 cup SUGAR

1 tsp. CINNAMON
1 cup ALL-PURPOSE FLOUR
1/2 cup BROWN SUGAR
1/2 tsp. SALT

Peel, core and dice apples and place in a large buttered baking dish. Pour juice over top and sprinkle with sugar. Blend cinnamon, flour, brown sugar and salt together. Sprinkle this mixture over apples. Bake in a 375° oven for 30 minutes or until topping is brown and apples are tender. Serves 6.

SWEET POTATO BANANA BREAKFAST

Sweet potatoes for breakfast? Try this recipe and you'll find out how great they can be!

1 can (23 oz.) whole SWEET POTATOES
1 Tbsp. CORNSTARCH
1/3 cup BROWN SUGAR, packed
1 cup ORANGE JUICE
1 Tbsp. BUTTER
1 Tbsp. ORANGE RIND, grated
3 med. BANANAS

Drain sweet potatoes, reserving syrup. Slice each sweet potato in half lengthwise and place in a single layer in a 1 1/2-quart baking dish. Stir together cornstarch, reserved syrup and brown sugar in small saucepan over medium heat. Gradually stir in orange juice. Stir constantly until clear and thickened. Remove from heat. Stir in butter and orange rind. Peel bananas and score by drawing a fork lengthwise down the sides. Slice crosswise into 1/4 inch slices. Arrange banana slices over sweet potatoes. Spoon orange sauce evenly over top. Bake in preheated oven at 400° for 15 minutes. Serves 6.

SWEET TATER CRISP

7 cups cooked and mashed
    SWEET POTATOES
3/4 cup SUGAR
1 stick BUTTER, melted
1 tsp. CINNAMON
2 EGGS, beaten

1/3 cup MILK
1 tsp. VANILLA
1 cup LIGHT BROWN SUGAR
1/2 cup ALL-PURPOSE
    FLOUR
1 cup chopped PECANS

In a large bowl, mix potatoes, sugar, half of butter, cinnamon, eggs, milk and vanilla until smooth. In a separate bowl, mix together the brown sugar and flour. Blend balance of butter into flour mixture. Add pecans and stir. Place sweet potato mixture in a large baking dish and cover with brown sugar mixture. Bake in a 350° oven for 30 minutes. Serves 10.

TUMBLEWEED FRUIT PIZZA

2 1/2 cups BUTTERMILK BAKING MIX
1/2 cup MILK
3 Tbsp. BUTTER, melted
1 pkg. (8 oz.) CREAM CHEESE,
    softened
1 tsp. SUGAR
1 tsp. VANILLA
1 APPLE, cored and thinly
    sliced
1 BANANA, peeled and sliced
1 PEACH, pitted and sliced
1 ORANGE, peeled and sliced
1 KIWI FRUIT, peeled and sliced
1/2 cup STRAWBERRIES, hulled and sliced

Mix buttermilk baking mix with milk and butter into a soft dough. Spread the dough evenly to the edges of a round, ungreased pizza pan. Bake at 425° for 15 minutes, remove from oven to cool. Combine the cream cheese, sugar and vanilla. Spread cream cheese mixture over the surface of the crust. Spread sliced fruits over top in a colorful arrangement and top with *Tumbleweed Fruit Glaze.*

TUMBLEWEED FRUIT GLAZE

2/3 cup SUGAR   2 Tbsp. CORNSTARCH
1/4 tsp. SALT   1 cup ORANGE JUICE

In a saucepan, combine all ingredients and boil for one minute. Let cool before spreading over fruit.

CHORIZO CASSEROLE

Compliments of Charlie and Mary J. Bast, Innkeepers, White Mountain Lodge, Greer, Arizona. "If you don't add the chorizo, this makes a great vegetarian dish!"

8 slices of BREAD, cubed into 1-inch pieces
1/3 cup chopped ONIONS
1 1/2 cups CHEDDAR CHEESE
1 1/2 cups MONTEREY JACK CHEESE
1 can (4 oz.) diced GREEN CHILES
1 lb. CHORIZO, cooked and drained
2 cups MILK
6 EGGS
1/2 tsp. ground MUSTARD
4-6 drops TABASCO® SAUCE
garlic and ground PEPPER to taste

In order given, layer first 6 ingredients in a 9 x 13 greased casserole dish. Combine together the remaining ingredients and pour over the layers in the casserole. Cover and refrigerate 8 hours or overnight. Bake in a preheated 350° oven for 1 hour or until mixture is set. Let stand for 15 minutes before dividing into serving size pieces.

BAGEL RANCHO

Recipes on this page compliments of Elin Jeffords, Phoenix, Arizona. Elin is a celebrated restaurant reviewer, consultant and author.

1 plain BAGEL
1/8 lb. BRIE, room temperature
2 lg. slices TOMATO
4 slices SMOKED SALMON
2 Tbsp. chopped GREEN CHILES
freshly ground BLACK PEPPER

Split and toast bagels. Spread each half with brie. Layer halves with tomato slices, salmon, and green chiles. Dust liberally with black pepper. Serves 1.

CONFETTI CASSEROLE

1 pkg. (24 oz.) frozen HASH BROWNS, thawed
2 cups grated MONTEREY JACK or CHEDDAR CHEESE
1 can (4 oz.) diced GREEN CHILES
1 cup cooked, diced HAM or SAUSAGE
1 RED BELL PEPPER, seeded and sliced into six rings
6 EGGS
freshly ground BLACK PEPPER

Grease a 13 x 9 x 2 baking dish. Combine hash browns, cheese, chiles and ham and place in baking dish. Arrange pepper rings over top and crack one egg into each. Bake in a preheated 400° oven for 20 minutes or until eggs are done. Serves 3 to 6.

MICROWAVE MIGAS

1 tsp. BUTTER
4 EGGS
4 Tbsp. PICANTE sauce
1 cup roughly crushed TORTILLA CHIPS
1/2 cup grated CHEDDAR or MONTEREY JACK CHEESE
SALT and PEPPER to taste

Put butter in a microwave pan and melt (about 25-50 seconds). Scramble in eggs and picante sauce. Cook about one minute and stir. Continue cooking and stirring at 25 second intervals until eggs are just a little runny. Turn in tortilla chips and cheese, cook a few more seconds until texture is firm and cheese melted. Season to taste with salt and pepper. Serves 2.

APPLE OATCAKES

Compliments of Campbell's Resort, Chelan, Washington.

1 1/2 cups WHEAT FLOUR
1 1/4 cups WHITE FLOUR
1 cup GROUND OATMEAL
1 Tbsp. BAKING POWDER
4 tsp. BAKING SODA
1 tsp. SALT
1/4 lb. BUTTER
6 EGGS
1 qt. BUTTERMILK
1/2 cup HONEY
1/4 cup diced YELLOW APPLE, BLUEBERRIES or RAISINS

Mix first 6 ingredients and then cut in butter in a food processor or with a pastry cutter. Add eggs, buttermilk and honey. Sprinkle apples on oatcakes before flipping over on grill. These take a little longer than a regular hotcake and tend to be a little darker. Blueberries or raisins may be substituted for apples, if you wish.

TASTY MEXICAN EGGS

Compliments of Patricia Martin, Twin Trees Bed & Breakfast, Jackson, Wyoming. Pat says, "This recipe is a favorite with our guests."

1 English-style MUFFIN, preferably cinnamon-raisin
1 AVOCADO, mashed
2 EGGS, poached or scrambled
SALSA
grated MONTEREY JACK CHEESE

Toast muffin lightly. Spread avocado on each half. Place a poached egg on each half (or split the scrambled eggs between them). Top each egg with a tablespoon of salsa and sprinkle with cheese. Place in a baking pan and broil 3 inches below broiling element. Cook until eggs are done, cheese is bubbly and muffin edges start to brown. Serves 1.

BANANA PECAN PANCAKES

Compliments of the Shelburne Inn, Seaview, Washington.

2 BANANAS
2 EGGS
3 cups BUTTERMILK
3 Tbsp. BUTTER, melted
2 cups UNBLEACHED
    WHITE FLOUR
1 tsp. BAKING SODA

1/2 tsp. SALT
1 cup CORNMEAL
1/2 cup BRAN
1 Tbsp. HONEY
1/2 cup PECANS
    (sautéed in butter)

In a medium bowl, mash the bananas with a fork until the lumps are mostly worked out. Add eggs, buttermilk and melted butter. Mix thoroughly. In a separate bowl, sift the flour with the baking soda and salt, then stir in the bran and cornmeal. Add the dry ingredients to the banana mixture, stirring until the dry ingredients are moistened. Add the nuts and honey and cook the pancakes just as you would any other. Serve with homemade *Cranberry Orange Sauce* or see Toppings Section (pages 79-82)

CRANBERRY ORANGE SAUCE

24 oz. fresh CRANBERRIES
1 1/2 cups WATER
2 cups SUGAR
1/2 cup DRY WHITE WINE

1 ORANGE (include juice
    and grated rind)
1 stick CINNAMON

In a saucepan, add the sugar to the water and bring to a boil. Add cranberries and remaining ingredients. Return to a boil, lower heat and cook for 15-20 minutes. Remove the cinnamon stick and strain mixture, reserving the liquid. Place the ingredients from the sieve in a food processor and process for one minute. Pour this mixture and reserved liquid into a saucepan along with the cinnamon stick and simmer for 15 minutes to thicken.

BREAKFAST CASSEROLE

Compliments of Cindy Barnes, Cindy's Creations, Sheridan, Wyoming. Cindy is a food caterer who lives in Sheridan. This is one of her favorite breakfast recipes.

1 pkg. (10 oz.) frozen POTATO CHUNKS, thawed
1/2 cup BUTTER, melted
12 EGGS, beaten
1 cup MILK
2 cups grated CHEESE (your choice)
1/2 cup any VEGETABLE or 1/2 cup combination of chopped
     ONION, GREEN BELL PEPPER, sliced MUSHROOMS, sliced
     BLACK OLIVES and diced CHILE PEPPERS
1 cup cooked: SAUSAGE, HAM (diced), or BACON (crumbled)

Place potatoes in a 9 x 13 baking dish and pour melted butter over top. Broil until brown crust forms. Beat together the eggs and milk and combine with cheese, vegetables and meat. Pour over potato mixture and cover with foil. Bake at 350° for 45 minutes. Serve with salsa on the side.

SWISS CHEESE & EGGS

1 Tbsp. BUTTER
1 lb. sliced SWISS CHEESE
8 EGGS
SALT and PEPPER to taste
2/3 cup HEAVY CREAM
1/3 cup grated SWISS CHEESE

Butter the bottom of a shallow baking dish. Layer dish with sliced Swiss cheese and break eggs over top. Sprinkle eggs with salt and pepper and pour cream over all. Sprinkle with grated Swiss cheese and bake at 350° for 15-20 minutes. Serves 4.

GRANDMA'S BISCUITS & GRAVY

Biscuits:
  2 1/2 cups ALL-PURPOSE FLOUR
  1/8 cup SUGAR
  1 tsp. BAKING POWDER
  1/2 tsp. BAKING SODA
  1/2 tsp. SALT
  1 tsp. DRY YEAST
  1/2 cup SHORTENING
  1 cup BUTTERMILK

Gravy:
  1 1/2 lbs. GROUND
    SAUSAGE
  4 heaping Tbsp.
    FLOUR
  1/2 can EVAPORATED MILK
  1/2 can WATER
  2 cups MILK
  SALT and PEPPER to taste

Grandma, you're the best!

Combine all dry ingredients, cut in shortening with pastry blender until thoroughly combined. Stir in buttermilk just until blended. Place dough on a floured board, knead gently and pat out to 1/2-inch thickness. Cut into rounds. Bake 10-12 minutes at 400°. Meanwhile, brown sausage over medium heat; add flour, stirring to brown lightly. Slowly add combined evaporated milk and water. Cook 1-2 minutes. Slowly add remaining milk and cook until thickened to taste. Stir in salt and pepper.

RICOTTA PANCAKES

Compliments of Turtleback Farm Inn, Orcas Island, Washington.

3 EGGS, separated
1 cup RICOTTA CHEESE
2/3 cup MILK
1/4 cup WHITE FLOUR
1/4 cup WHOLE WHEAT FLOUR
1 tsp. BAKING POWDER
1 pinch SALT

Beat egg whites until stiff, but not dry. To the yolks, add remaining ingredients, blending until thoroughly mixed. Fold the whites into the batter. Bake on a greased, hot griddle until golden brown. Serve with butter and syrup or honey or one of the toppings in Toppings Section (see pages 79-82).

SPICED WAFFLES

Compliments of Turtleback Farm Inn, Orcas Island, Washington.

2 cups BUTTERMILK
6 Tbsp. BUTTER, melted, cooled
2 EGGS, separated
1 cup WHOLE WHEAT FLOUR
3/4 cup WHITE FLOUR
1/4 cup ROLLED OATS or
    OAT FLOUR

2 tsp. BAKING POWDER
1 tsp. SODA
1/2 tsp. SALT
1 Tbsp. SUGAR
1/2 tsp. CINNAMON
1/4 tsp. NUTMEG
1/2 tsp. ALLSPICE

In a bowl, blend together buttermilk, butter and egg yolks. Sift dry ingredients together and blend into buttermilk mixture. Fold in beaten whites (beaten stiff but not dry), until just blended. Bake waffles and serve with butter and honey blended together in equal amounts, to which a little orange zest has been added.

BREAKFAST CREPES

6 Tbsp. BUTTER	1 cup WATER
6 EGGS, slightly beaten	1 1/2 cups FLOUR
1 cup MILK	1/2 tsp. SALT

Melt butter in a 10-inch omelet pan (or 8-inch crepe pan). Pour melted butter into mixing bowl; add eggs, milk and water and beat together with rotary beater. Blend in flour and salt until mixture is smooth. Heat buttered omelet pan until just hot enough to sizzle a drop of water. For each crepe, pour scant 1/4 cup batter into pan (rotating pan as batter is poured). Cook until lightly browned on bottom; remove from pan or turn and brown other side. (Crepes should set to a thin, lacy pancake almost immediately. If too much batter is poured into pan, pour off excess immediately.) Stack between sheets of paper toweling or waxed paper until ready to use. (Crepes may be frozen.) Spread *Crepe Filling* on each crepe; roll up, and serve 3 crepes per person. (Makes about 20 crepes.)

CREPE FILLING

2 cans (13 1/2 oz. ea.) PINEAPPLE TIDBITS, well drained
3 cups MANDARIN ORANGE SEGMENTS
1 cup FLAKE COCONUT
1 cup SOUR CREAM

Combine all ingredients. Chill to blend flavors.

A gourmet good morning!

BREAKFAST FRY BREAD TACO

Compliments of John Kingsmore, Executive Chef at the El Tovar Hotel at the Grand Canyon.

3/4 cup MILK
1/4 cup SUGAR
2 tsp. SALT
4 1/2 Tbsp. SHORTENING
3/4 cup WARM WATER

1 pkg. YEAST
2 1/4 cups ALL-PURPOSE
   FLOUR
2 1/4 cups FLOUR

In a saucepan, bring milk, sugar, salt and shortening to a simmer. Remove from heat and cool to room temperature. Place warm water and yeast in a bowl and add milk mixture. Add flour and mix until smooth. If sticky, add additional flour. On a bread board, work dough until smooth and elastic. Cover and let rise until double in volume. Punch down and divide into six equal pieces. Roll into circles. In a heavy pan, heat oil and fry dough circles. Arrange on a shallow baking pan.

Topping:
   12 EGGS, beaten
   6 oz. ROASTED JULIENNE PEPPERS
   12 oz. PULLED SMOKED CHICKEN MEAT
   6 oz. cooked BLACK BEANS
   12 EGGS, beaten
   12 oz. JALAPEÑO JACK CHEESE, grated

In a skillet, sauté roasted peppers, chicken and black beans. Add eggs and cook until all are just bound. Place egg mixture on top of dough rings and top with cheese. Flash under broiler to melt cheese and then cut into quarters.

SWEETS

SUNRISE PUDDING

3 PEARS, cored and diced
1/4 cup LEMON JUICE
2 cups BREAD CUBES
1/3 cup BUTTER, melted
1/4 cup SUGAR

1/2 tsp. SALT
1/4 tsp. ALLSPICE
1/4 tsp. CINNAMON
1/2 cup RAISINS

Combine and fold all ingredients together. Place in a greased 2-quart casserole. Cover and bake at 350° for 20 minutes. Remove cover and bake 15 minutes longer. Serve warm with honey on the side or see Toppings Section (pages 79-82). Serves 4.

BREAKFAST PUDDING

4 slices WHITE BREAD
BUTTER, softened
5 EGGS
1 1/2 cups MILK
1 tsp. DRY MUSTARD

1 tsp SALT
1/2 tsp. DRIED ONION
1 cup grated CHEDDAR
   CHEESE
1 Tbsp. BLACK PEPPER

Butter bread slices on both sides and place in a large baking pan. Beat eggs, milk, dry mustard, salt and dried onion together. Pour liquid mixture over bread. Sprinkle cheese and pepper over the top and cover. Place in refrigerator for 4 hours. Bake at 350° for 30 minutes. Serves 6.

ORANGE SUNSHINE

4 EGGS, beaten
1 cup LIGHT CREAM
1 cup ORANGE JUICE
1/2 tsp. grated ORANGE PEEL
3/4 cup SUGAR

1/2 tsp. NUTMEG
1/2 tsp. VANILLA
2 tsp. BUTTER
sliced ORANGE

Combine all ingredients except butter in a saucepan. Stir over low heat for 5 minutes until mixture thickens. Remove from heat and stir in the butter. When butter has melted, pour mixture into individual fruit cups and chill for 2 hours, or overnight. Garnish with orange slices and serve. Serves 4.

SWEET POTATO PUDDING

3 cups cooked and mashed SWEET POTATOES
1 stick BUTTER
6 large MARSHMALLOWS
2 EGGS
1 1/2 cups SUGAR
1 tsp. VANILLA
1/4 tsp. SALT

In a large bowl, combine all ingredients and stir until well-blended. Place in a greased baking dish. Spread *Coconut Topping* over the top of sweet potato mixture. Bake in 350° oven for 30 minutes or until brown and bubbly. Serves 4.

COCONUT TOPPING

1 cup BROWN SUGAR
1 cup COCONUT FLAKES

1/2 stick BUTTER
1 cup chopped WALNUTS

Combine all ingredients together in a bowl.

RICE PUDDING

2 EGGS
1/2 cup SUGAR
1 tsp. SALT
1 1/2 cups MILK
1 Tbsp. VANILLA
2 cups cooked RICE
1 tsp. NUTMEG
1/2 cup RAISINS

In a large mixing bowl, beat eggs. Add remaining ingredients and combine. Pour into a greased, 2-quart casserole dish and bake at 325° for one hour. Serve warm with honey on the side or see Toppings Section (pages 79-82). Serves 4.

MEXICAN BREAD PUDDING

8 slices BREAD, toasted
3 EGGS, beaten
5 Tbsp. MILK
1 tsp. CINNAMON
2 Tbsp. BROWN SUGAR
1/2 cup slivered ALMONDS
1/2 cup chopped, unsalted PEANUTS
1/2 cup chopped WALNUTS
1/2 cup RAISINS
1 med. APPLE, cored and diced
1 cup MONTEREY JACK CHEESE, diced

Muy bueno!

Layer four toasted bread slices in a greased 9 x 9 baking dish. Mix together the eggs, milk, cinnamon, brown sugar, almonds, peanuts, walnuts, raisins, apple and cheese. Pour half of this mixture on top of bread slices. Add another layer of bread and pour in the remaining mixture. Pour *Brown Sugar Sauce* over top of pudding. Place in oven and bake in preheated 350° oven for 30 minutes. Serve warm. Serves 4.

BROWN SUGAR SAUCE

2 cups BROWN SUGAR
2 cups WATER
1 CINNAMON STICK

Combine brown sugar, water and cinnamon stick in a pan. Bring to a boil. Lower heat and let simmer for 15 minutes or until sauce is thickened. Remove the cinnamon stick.

WALNUTTY DATE CAKE

1 cup WATER
1 tsp. BAKING SODA
2 cups chopped DATES
1 Tbsp. BUTTER
1 tsp. VANILLA
1/2 cup chopped WALNUTS

1 1/2 cups WHOLE WHEAT
   FLOUR
1 cup BROWN SUGAR
1/2 tsp. CINNAMON
1/4 tsp. SALT
1 EGG

In a saucepan, bring water to a boil and add baking soda. Stir until dissolved. Add dates and butter and simmer until dates have melted. Remove from heat. Add vanilla and walnuts and let stand. Sift together flour, sugar, cinnamon and salt. Beat egg until fluffy and fold into flour mixture. Combine both mixtures until well blended. Pour into greased 9 x 9 pan and bake at 350° for one hour. Serve warm with **Honey Butter** (see page 81). Serves 4.

COWBOY BREAKFAST COOKIES

Come 'n' get em!

1/2 cup BUTTER, softened
3/4 cup SUGAR
1 EGG
1 cup ALL-PURPOSE FLOUR
1/4 tsp. BAKING SODA
1/2 cup BACON, cooked crisp
   and drained
2 cups CORNFLAKES
1/2 cup RAISINS
1/4 cup chopped WALNUTS

Cream butter and sugar together until fluffy. Add the egg, flour and baking soda. Crumble bacon into small pieces and combine with cornflakes, raisins and nuts. Add to butter mixture. Shape dough into 2-inch balls and place on an ungreased baking sheet. Bake in oven at 350° for 20 minutes.

ARIZONA COFFEE CAKE

1/4 lb. BUTTER, melted
2 EGGS
1 cup SUGAR
2 cups ALL-PURPOSE FLOUR
1 tsp. BAKING POWDER
2/3 cup MILK

1 tsp. SALT
1 tsp. grated ORANGE RIND
1 tsp. VANILLA
1/4 cup BUTTER, melted
1/2 cup SUGAR
3/4 cup ALL-PURPOSE FLOUR

In a large mixing bowl blend together butter, eggs and sugar. Slowly stir in flour until well blended. Add baking powder, milk, salt, orange rind and vanilla. Stir until completely blended. Pour into a 9 x 9 cake pan. Bake at 400° for 15 minutes. Spread a thin layer of melted butter over the top of the cake. Combine sugar and flour and sprinkle over butter. Bake an additional 30 minutes. Remove when top is a deep golden brown.

RAISIN PIE

1 lb. RAISINS
1 1/2 cups WATER
1/2 cup SUGAR
2 Tbsp. ALL-PURPOSE FLOUR
1 LEMON PEEL, shredded
1/2 cup COLD WATER
2 (9") uncooked PIE CRUSTS
1 Tbsp. SUGAR
1 Tbsp. MILK

Place water in a saucepan and bring to a boil. Add raisins and return to a boil. Remove from heat immediately. Set aside. In a bowl, mix sugar, flour and lemon peel together. Stir in cold water to make a smooth paste. Add sugar mixture to raisins and cook over moderate heat, stirring constantly, until thickened. Pour hot mixture into pastry shell, cover with top crust and flute the edges. Use a fork to poke several holes in top of crust. Mix together sugar and milk and brush on top of pie crust. Bake at 425° for 40 minutes.

RHUBARB APPLE COBBLER

1/2 cup SUGAR
2 Tbsp. CORNSTARCH
1 tsp. CINNAMON
2 cups chopped APPLES

2 cups chopped RHUBARB
1 Tbsp. WATER
2 Tbsp. BUTTER, melted

Combine sugar, cornstarch, cinnamon, apples, rhubarb and water in a large saucepan. Cook over medium heat, stirring often until mixture boils. Boil for one minute and then pour into a 9 x 12 baking dish. Brush melted butter over top and add spoonfuls of *Crumble Topping.* Bake in a 400° oven for 30 minutes.

CRUMBLE TOPPING

1 cup ALL-PURPOSE FLOUR
1/2 cup SUGAR
2 tsp. BAKING POWDER

1 tsp. SALT
1/3 cup MILK

Sift flour, sugar, baking powder and salt together. Add milk and mix gently until only small lumps remain.

COWBOY COFFEE CHOCOLATE PIE

1 cup BLACK COFFEE,
  strong blend
1/2 cup SUGAR
3/4 cup ground CHOCOLATE
4 EGGS, separated
1/2 cup WARM WATER

1 pkg. (1 oz.) unflavored
  GELATIN
1/2 cup SUGAR
1 baked PIE SHELL
NON-DAIRY TOPPING

Over low heat, mix together coffee, sugar, chocolate and egg yolks. While mixture is heating, dissolve gelatin in warm water. Combine with coffee mixture and stir until mixture starts to thicken. Beat four egg whites with 1/2 cup of sugar. Fold the chocolate mixture into the beaten egg whites. Pour mixture into a baked pie shell and chill for 4 hours. Serve with dollops of non-dairy topping.

OLD-FASHIONED SOPAIPILLAS

Sopaipillas can be eaten any time of the day, but they're especially perfect for breakfasts and brunches!

4 cups ALL-PURPOSE FLOUR
1 tsp. SALT
4 tsp. BAKING POWDER
4 Tbsp. SHORTENING

2 EGGS, beaten
1/2 cup SUGAR
MILK
OIL for deep frying

Sift the flour, salt and baking powder together into a bowl. Add shortening, eggs and sugar and mix until well blended. Add just enough milk to make a thick but still pliable dough. Let rest for 15 minutes. On a lightly floured board, divide dough in half and roll each half into circles that are 1/4-inch thick. Cut circles into quarters and fry in hot cooking oil until golden brown. Drain on paper towels and serve warm.

RISE & SHINE FRUIT MEDLEY

2 Tbsp. quick cooking TAPIOCA
2 1/2 cups ORANGE JUICE
2 Tbsp. SUGAR
1/2 tsp. SALT
2 CINNAMON STICKS
1 1/2 cups ORANGE SECTIONS
1 pkg. (12 oz.) frozen SLICED PEACHES, thawed
1 BANANA, sliced

Combine tapioca, orange juice, sugar and salt in a saucepan. Let stand for 5 minutes. Add cinnamon sticks. Bring mixture to a boil over medium heat. Remove from heat and let cool for 20 minutes. Remove cinnamon sticks and add peach and banana slices. Heat and serve. Serves 6.

CINNAMON CHURROS

This sweet treat comes from Mexico. The secret to the shape is the star-tip on the pastry bag.

1 cup ALL-PURPOSE FLOUR
1 tsp. CINNAMON
1 cup WATER
1/2 tsp. SALT
1 EGG, lightly beaten

1 slice BREAD
1/2 slice LEMON
OIL
POWDERED SUGAR

In a bowl, sift flour and cinnamon together four times. In a saucepan, bring water to a boil and add salt. Pour boiling water all at once over flour mixture, stirring vigorously to a fluffy batter. Add egg and continue beating until mixture is shiny. Place batter in a pastry bag with a large star-tip. Add 1 inch of oil to a large skillet and heat to 375°. Holding bag about 1 inch over oil, gently squeeze out four-inch pieces of batter into oil. Fry until golden brown. Remove and drain on paper towels. Sift powdered sugar over churros while they are warm and place on serving plate.

SUNNY FRUIT SURPRISE FOR A CROWD

1 can (29 oz.) RED PLUMS
1 can (29 oz.) FRUIT COCKTAIL
1 can (20 oz.) PINEAPPLE TIDBITS
1 can (16 oz.) SOUR RED CHERRIES
3/4 cup RAISINS
2 cups PINEAPPLE JUICE
1 cup ORANGE JUICE
1 ORANGE, thinly sliced
1 LEMON, thinly sliced
1 pkg. (3 oz.) CHERRY GELATIN
3 Tbsp. quick cooking TAPIOCA

Where'd they all come from?

In a large saucepan, combine the undrained canned fruits and remaining ingredients. Mix well and heat to boiling point. Let simmer 15 minutes. Serve either warm or cold.

OLD-FASHIONED FLAN

Flan is generally served as a dessert, but many families serve it for breakfasts, too! Try this recipe and you might discover a new morning favorite!

1 cup SUGAR
1 can (14 oz.) SWEETENED
   CONDENSED MILK
1 can (5 oz.) EVAPORATED
   MILK

1 cup WHIPPING CREAM
4 WHOLE EGGS
2 EGG YOLKS
1 CINNAMON STICK

Preheat oven to 325°. Place sugar in a small skillet and heat over medium-high heat. When sugar begins to melt, reduce heat to medium. Continue to cook, stirring occasionally, until sugar is melted. Immediately pour into a 2-quart baking dish, tilting to coat bottom and sides completely. Combine condensed milk, evaporated milk, cream and eggs in blender. Process until thoroughly mixed. Pour into baking dish lined with caramelized sugar. Drop cinnamon stick into middle of mixture. Set baking dish in a larger baking pan. Pour hot water into the bottom pan halfway up the sides of the baking dish. Cover loosely with foil and bake about 1 1/2 hours or until a knife inserted near center comes out clean. Remove dish from hot water and place on a rack to cool. Refrigerate for several hours. To remove from dish, run a knife around the top edge, place a serving plate with a rim over dish and invert. Scrape all of the remaining sauce from dish and spoon over flan. Makes 8 servings.

SUN VALLEY ORANGE PARFAIT

1 1/2 cups COTTAGE CHEESE, creamed
2 Tbsp. frozen ORANGE JUICE CONCENTRATE, thawed
2 cups ORANGE and GRAPEFRUIT SECTIONS

In a small bowl, mix together the cottage cheese and orange juice concentrate. In parfait glasses, alternately layer orange and grapefruit sections and cottage cheese mixture, ending with a fruit layer. Chill for one hour and serve. Serves 4.

BREAKFAST TOPPINGS

CARAMEL TOPPING

2 cups BROWN SUGAR   **1/2 cup EVAPORATED MILK**
1/2 cup BUTTER   **1 1/2 tsp. VANILLA**

Combine sugar, butter and milk in a saucepan. Place over medium heat, bring to a boil for 5 minutes, stirring occasionally. Remove from heat, add vanilla and beat to desired spreading consistency.

ORANGE TOPPING

1/2 cup POWDERED SUGAR   **2 tsp. ORANGE JUICE**
1 tsp. grated ORANGE PEEL

Combine and drizzle over hot breakfast treats.

TOASTED ALMOND TOPPING

1/4 cup SUGAR   **2 1/2 tsp. ORANGE LIQUEUR**
1/2 cup ORANGE JUICE   **1/2 cup toasted ALMONDS**

Combine all ingredients and pour over hot breakfast treats.

APPLE BUTTER

1 cup dried APPLE SLICES
3 cups WARM WATER
1/2 cup GRAPEFRUIT sections
1/4 cup ORANGE sections
1 1/3 cups SUGAR

Wash apples and place in warm water. Cover and let stand for at least eight hours. Place in a saucepan over moderate heat and simmer until apples are soft. Add fruit sections and sugar to saucepan. Simmer until mixture thickens. Pour into sterile jars and seal according to manufacturer's instructions.

APPLE-DATE JAM

2 cups chopped APPLES
2 cups chopped DATES
3/4 cup APPLE JUICE

Place all ingredients in a saucepan and boil until mixture is very thick. Pour into sterile jars and seal according to manufacturers instructions.

BUTTERSCOTCH GLAZE

1 cup SUGAR
1/2 cup BUTTERMILK
1/2 tsp. BAKING SODA
1/2 tsp. VANILLA
1/4 cup MARGARINE
1/4 cup CORN SYRUP

Place all ingredients in a saucepan. Bring to a boil and continue boiling, stirring constantly, for 10 minutes. Pour hot over puddings, pancakes, rolls or cakes.

BROWN SUGAR SYRUP

2 cups BROWN SUGAR
1 cup WHITE CORN SYRUP
1 EGG
1/2 cup MILK
1 tsp. CINNAMON
1 tsp. VANILLA

In medium size saucepan, combine brown sugar and corn syrup. Bring to a boil. Beat egg, milk, cinnamon and vanilla together. Add to the syrup mixture slowly, stirring constantly. Bring syrup mixture to a boil again. Remove from heat. Serve warm or cold over your favorite pancakes, waffles, toast, and even ice cream or yogurt!

ORANGE SAUCE

1/4 cup BUTTER, melted
2 EGGS, beaten
2 Tbsp. grated ORANGE PEEL
1/3 cup ORANGE JUICE
1/4 cup SUGAR
1 Tbsp. grated LEMON PEEL
2 Tbsp. LEMON JUICE

This is my favorite!

Combine all ingredients in a small saucepan. Mix until smooth. Cook over a medium heat, stirring constantly until thick and creamy. Remove from heat and serve with waffles, pancakes, toast and other breakfast treats. Makes one cup of sauce.

HONEY BUTTER

1/2 cup BUTTER
1/4 cup HONEY

1 tsp. CINNAMON
1 tsp. VANILLA

In a small mixing bowl, cream butter until fluffy. Gradually add honey while still mixing. When mixture is smooth, add cinnamon and vanilla. Store in refrigerator until ready to use.

CREAMY NUT TOPPING

1/2 cup packed BROWN SUGAR
2 Tbsp. FLOUR
1/2 cup EVAPORATED MILK
2 Tbsp. BUTTER

1/3 cup finely chopped
   WALNUTS or PECANS
1/2 tsp. VANILLA
dash SALT

In a medium saucepan, stir together the brown sugar, flour and milk. Add butter and cook, stirring constantly, until mixture is thickened and bubbly. Remove from heat and stir in nuts, vanilla and salt. Great on pancakes, sweet rolls, puddings and sopaipillas.

POWDERED SUGAR FROSTING

1 EGG WHITE
1/2 cup SHORTENING
1/4 cup BUTTER

1 tsp. VANILLA
2 cups sifted POWDERED
   SUGAR

In a mixer bowl, beat together the egg white, shortening, butter and vanilla at medium speed until well blended. Gradually add powdered sugar, beating until light and fluffy.

GINGER-NUT TOPPING

1/2 cup BROWN SUGAR
3/4 tsp. CINNAMON
1/4 tsp. GINGER

6 Tbsp. BUTTER
1/2 cup chopped WALNUTS

Combine brown sugar, cinnamon and ginger together. Cut in butter until mixture is crumbly. Stir in walnuts. Sprinkle topping on pancakes, puddings, waffles or any of your favorite breakfast treats.

BREAKFAST DRINKS

Mighty good!

CAMPFIRE COFFEE

If you wanta make coffee, cowboy brew

I'm gonna tell you what to do.

Use your own brand of grounds—your regular stuff,

Pour in cold water, till you've got enough.

Now boil that pot for an hour or so,

Over an open campfire, don'tcha know.

Throw in some egg shells for an authentic taste,

Call all your cowboys—don't let this go to waste.

Now take the pot off the fire and let cool awhile,

And when they taste it, just watch them smile!

Bruce Fischer

COWBOY COFFEE

4 qt. WATER
1 1/2 cups freshly ground COFFEE
1 EGG SHELL
1/2 cup COLD WATER

Bring water to a boil in a large saucepan or coffee pot. Add coffee grounds and egg shell to boiling water. Return to a boil, then remove from heat and let stand for 2 minutes. Slowly add cold water to settle grounds to the bottom. Strain if desired.

ORANGE PUDDING DRINK

1 Tbsp. VANILLA PUDDING MIX
3 Tbsp. SUGAR
1 cup ORANGE JUICE
1 cup WATER
1/2 cup ICE

Mix pudding, sugar, juice, water and ice in a blender. Blend at low speed for about one minute and then blend for two minutes on high speed. Serve cold. Serves one.

SUNNY ARIZONA TEA

The strength of the tea depends on how long you leave it in the sun.

1 gal. COLD WATER
8 TEA BAGS
2 Tbsp. LEMON JUICE

In a large sterilized jar, place water and tea bags. Cover and set outdoors in full sunlight for 4 to 6 hours. Stir in lemon juice, pour over ice in glasses and serve with lemon wedges. Add honey to sweeten.

ORANGE-BRANDY PUNCH

A special adults-only treat for cold winter weekends!

rind of 1 ORANGE
4 sticks CINNAMON
2 whole CLOVES

6 cubes SUGAR
1/2 cup warm BRANDY
4 cups hot COFFEE

Cut the rind of the orange into thin strips and place in a baking dish. Add cinnamon, cloves and sugar. Pour in warm brandy and carefully light with a match. Stir ingredients until flames are gone and sugar cubes are dissolved. Add hot coffee and mix until blended. Serve in demitasse cups. Makes one quart.

BANANA-ORANGE MILK

6 Tbsp. frozen ORANGE JUICE CONCENTRATE, thawed
1 cup COLD WATER
1 cup MILK
1 BANANA
1 cup CORN FLAKES
1 Tbsp. SUGAR

Combine the orange juice concentrate, water, milk, banana, corn flakes and sugar in a blender. Cover and blend at high speed until smooth. Serves 2.

APPLE CIDER PUNCH

*Great for cold winter mornings. This punch warms you up
from the inside!*

**4 qts. APPLE JUICE
1 can (6 oz.) frozen LEMONADE
2 qts. CRANBERRY JUICE
1 tsp. WHOLE CLOVES
10 WHOLE ALLSPICE BERRIES
4 CINNAMON STICKS**

In a crock pot, combine apple juice, lemonade and cranberry
juice. Place a tea ball filled with the cloves and allspice in crock pot.
Add cinnamon sticks and heat on medium setting for 6 hours.
Serves 6 to 8.

MEXICAN
HOT CHOCOLATE MIX

*Compliments of Charlie & Mary J. Bast, Innkeepers, White Moun-
tain Lodge, Greer, Arizona. "I keep this mix on hand for cold, snowy
winter mornings—our guests ask for it often."*

Buenos días!

**1/2 cup COCOA
1 cup SUGAR
1/8 tsp. ALLSPICE
1 tsp. CINNAMON
1 tsp. NUTMEG
1/4 tsp. SALT
1 tsp. POWDERED VANILLA
1 1/2 cups POWDERED MILK**

Combine all ingredients well and store in an airtight container.
To use, add 1/8 cup of mix to 6 ounces of hot water. Top with a
dollop of whipping cream.

ORANGE-CARROT DRINK

2 CARROTS, peeled and diced
1 1/2 cups ORANGE JUICE
1 1/2 cups LOW-FAT MILK
1/4 cup HONEY

Combine carrots with balance of ingredients in blender. Cover and process at high speed until carrot is liquefied. Serve immediately. Makes 1 quart.

LOW-FAT ORANGE SHAKE

1 can (6 oz.) frozen ORANGE JUICE CONCENTRATE, thawed
1 1/2 cups VANILLA ICE MILK
2 1/4 cups SKIM MILK
4 scoops VANILLA ICE MILK

Combine orange juice concentrate with 1 1/2 cups ice milk and skim milk in blender. Cover and process at high speed until smooth. Pour into four glasses, top with scoops of vanilla ice milk. Serves 4.

ICY ORANGE SHRUB

1 pint LEMON SHERBET
1/4 cup APRICOT PRESERVES
1 can (6 oz.) frozen ORANGE JUICE CONCENTRATE, thawed
crushed ICE

Soften sherbet and blend with preserves. Stir in orange juice concentrate. Fill eight large glasses with crushed ice. Add lemon/orange mixture and stir.

HOT DESERT TEA

1/3 cup SUGAR
3 TEA BAGS
12 whole CLOVES
1 stick CINNAMON
1 strip fresh ORANGE PEEL
3 cups boiling WATER
1/2 cup fresh ORANGE JUICE
3 Tbsp. LEMON JUICE
LEMON SLICES, studded with WHOLE CLOVES

Place sugar, tea bags, spices and orange peel in a saucepan and pour boiling water over top. Steep for five minutes and then strain mixture. Stir in orange and lemon juices. Heat, but do not boil. Serve in cups garnished with lemon slices studded with whole cloves. Serves 4.

APPLE COOLER

3 GOLDEN DELICIOUS APPLES,
   peeled, cored, finely chopped
1/2 cup WATER

2 Tbsp. LEMON JUICE
2 cups ROSÉ WINE
2 cups CLUB SODA

In a saucepan, simmer apples, water and lemon juice for 20 minutes or until mixture has consistency of applesauce. Purée in blender or food processor. Cool to room temperature. To serve, combine equal parts of apple purée, wine and soda in six ice-filled glasses.

INDEX

(continued next page)

Brunch Recipes

Brunch Recipes (continued)

Cereals

(continued next page)

(continued next page)

Toppings (continued next page)

INDEX (continued)

ABOUT THE AUTHORS

Bruce Fischer is a native of Phoenix, Arizona and an enthusiastic Southwestern traveler. As avid hikers, Bruce and his wife, Bobbi, have traveled throughout the West collecting recipes from friendly people they meet along the way.

Bobbi Fischer, originally from Boston, has an enduring love affair with the Southwest. She is passionate about Mexican food and loves trying out new recipes. Bobbi has also authored more than 20 children's books.

Together they continue to test new recipes, take innovative cooking classes and add to their own cookbook collection.

*(See next page for additional
cookbooks by Bruce and Bobbi!)*

More Books by Bruce & Bobbi Fischer

TORTILLA LOVERS COOK BOOK

From tacos to tostadas, enchiladas to nachos, every dish celebrates the tortilla! More than 100 easy to prepare, festive recipes for breakfast, lunch and dinner. Filled with Southwestern flavors!

5 1/2 x 8 1/2 — 112 pages . . . $6.95

GRAND CANYON COOK BOOK

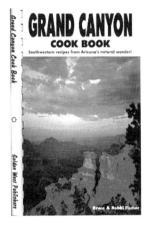

Inspired by the beauty of the Grand Canyon, this delicious collection of Southwestern recipes creates a natural wonder in the kitchen, too! Appetizers, beverages, breads, main dishes, desserts and lots more! Includes interesting Canyon facts and history.

5 1/2 x 8 1/2 — 120 pages . . . $6.95

UTAH COOK BOOK

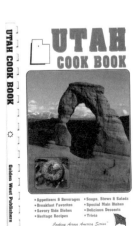

Packed with mouth-watering recipes such as *Stuffed Beef and Black Bean Tamale Pie* and *Cache Valley Cheese Soufflé*. Includes recipes using the official state cooking pot, the Dutch Oven. Includes information on the 2002 Olympic Winter Games and fascinating Utah trivia.

5 1/2 x 8 1/2 — 96 pages . . . $6.95

ORDER BLANK

GOLDEN WEST PUBLISHERS

☼ 4113 N. Longview Ave. • Phoenix, AZ 85014

www.goldenwestpublishers.com • **1-800-658-5830** • FAX 602-279-6901

Qty	Title	Price	Amount
	Arizona Cook Book	5.95	
	Arizona Territory Cook Book	6.95	
	Billy the Kid Cook Book	7.95	
	Chili-Lovers' Cook Book	5.95	
	Christmas in Arizona Cook Book	9.95	
	Christmas in Colorado Cook Book	9.95	
	Christmas in New Mexico Cook Book	9.95	
	Citrus Lovers Cook Book	6.95	
	Cowboy Cartoon Cook Book	7.95	
	Grand Canyon Cook Book	6.95	
	Kokopelli's Cook Book	9.95	
	Low Fat Mexican Recipes	6.95	
	Salsa Lovers Cook Book	5.95	
	Sedona Cook Book	7.95	
	Tequila Cook Book	7.95	
	Take This Chile and Stuff It!	6.95	
	Tortilla Lovers Cook Book	6.95	
	Utah Cook Book	6.95	
	Western Breakfasts	7.95	
	Wholly Frijoles The Whole Bean Cook Book	6.95	
Shipping & Handling Add ⫸	U.S. & Canada	$3.00	
	Other countries	$5.00	

☐ My Check or Money Order Enclosed $

☐ MasterCard   ☐ VISA ($20 credit card minimum)

_____

(Payable in U.S. funds)

Acct. No.   Exp. Date

Signature

Name   Telephone

Address

City/State/Zip
6/00   **Call for a FREE catalog of all of our titles**   Western Breakfasts

This order blank may be photo-copied.